# RISK-TAKING
## IS
# BIBLICAL

# RISK-TAKING IS BIBLICAL

## WHAT THE BIBLE TELLS US ABOUT PURSUING KINGDOM BUILDING

**MATTHEW CHANG**
**Foreword by Pastor Joby Martin**

**Chang Robotics**
**Jacksonville Beach, Florida**

*Risk-Taking Is Biblical* copyright © 2025 by Matthew Chang

All rights reserved. No part of this publication may be reproduced, distributed, or transmitted in any form or by any means, including photocopying, recording, or other electronic or mechanical methods, without the prior written permission of the publisher, except in the case of brief quotations embodied in critical reviews and certain other noncommercial uses permitted by copyright law. For permission requests, write to the publisher at the address below.

Chang Robotics
420 3rd Ave S, Jacksonville Beach, FL 32250
(904) 545-9059
www.changrobotics.ai

The conversations in the book are based on the author's recollections, though they are not intended to represent word-for-word transcripts. Rather, the author has retold them in a way that communicates the meaning of what was said. In the author's humble opinion, the essence of the dialogue is accurate in all instances.

Publisher's Cataloging-In-Publication Data

Names: Chang, Matthew, author. | Martin, Joby, writer of foreword.
Title: Risk-taking is biblical : what the Bible tells us about pursuing kingdom building / Matthew Chang; foreword by Pastor Joby Martin.
Description: Jacksonville Beach, FL : Chang Robotics, [2025] | Includes bibliographical references.
Identifiers: ISBN: 9798993115719 (hardcover) | 9798993115702 (softcover) | 9798993115726 (ebook) |
9798993115733 (audiobook)
Subjects: LCSH: Leadership--Biblical teaching. | Risk-taking (Psychology)--Biblical teaching. |
Entrepreneurship--Biblical teaching. | Christian leadership. | Christian life. | Kingdom of God.
Classification: LCC: BV4597.53.L43 C43 2025 | DDC: 158.4--dc23

I'd like to dedicate this book to my wife, Jamie, who has blessed me with a rich marriage, with encouragement to take risks and step out of my comfort zone, and with four beautiful children. I love you, Jamie; thank you for being my wing-woman. Also to my mother and father, Melody and Mario, who worked so hard to raise me and my brothers. My parents set the perfect example of what faith and hard work looked like—love you, Mom and Dad!

# The Parable of the Talents

14 "For it is just like a man about to go on a journey, who called his own slaves and entrusted his possessions to them. 15 To one he gave five [a]talents, to another, two, and to another, one, each according to his own ability; and he went on his journey. 16 The one who had received the five talents immediately went and did business with them, and earned five more talents. 17 In the same way the one who had received the two talents earned two more. 18 But he who received the one talent went away and dug a hole in the ground, and hid his [b]master's money.

19 "Now after a long time the master of those slaves *came and *settled accounts with them. 20 The one who had received the five talents came up and brought five more talents, saying, 'Master, you entrusted five talents to me. See, I have earned five more talents.' 21 His master said to him, 'Well done, good and faithful slave. You were faithful with a few things, I will put you in charge of many things; enter the joy of your [c]master.'

22 "Also the one who had received the two talents came up and said, 'Master, you entrusted two talents to me. See, I have earned two more talents.' 23 His master said to him, 'Well done, good and faithful slave. You were faithful with a few things, I will put you in charge of many things; enter the joy of your master.'

24 "Now the one who had received the one talent also came up and said, 'Master, I knew you to be a hard man, reaping where you did not sow, and gathering where you did not scatter seed. 25 And I was afraid, so I went away and hid your talent in the ground. See, you still have what is yours.'

26 "But his master answered and said to him, 'You [d]worthless, lazy slave! Did you know that I reap where I did not sow, and gather where I did not scatter seed? 27 Then you ought to have [e]put my money in the bank, and [f]on my arrival I would have received my money back with interest. 28 Therefore: take the talent away from him, and give it to the one who has the ten talents.'

29 "For to everyone who has, more shall be given, and he will have an abundance; but from the one who does not have, even what he does have shall be taken away. 30 And throw the worthless slave into the outer darkness; in that place there will be weeping and gnashing of teeth.

**Matthew 25:14-30**
**New American Standard Bible**

# Contents

Foreword by Pastor Joby Martin ..................................i

Chapter 1
The Kingdom Way ................................................1

Chapter 2
The State of Preparation ......................................27

Chapter 3
Study, Pray, Serve ..............................................47

Chapter 4
Start Small, Play Big ...........................................61

Chapter 5
Accumulate Wise Mentors ....................................77

Chapter 6
Network Aggressively .........................................93

Chapter 7
Build Your Team ...............................................105

Chapter 8
Become Financially Literate Biblically .....................125

Chapter 9
Parable of the Risks ..........................................133

Chapter 10
The Integrity Integer ........................................139

**Chapter 11**
**Christian Principles When the Going Gets Tough ........ 145**

**Chapter 12**
**Play It Forward ................................................................. 149**

**Appendix ........................................................................... 155**
**Acknowledgments ............................................................ 159**
**About the Author ............................................................. 161**

# **Foreword** by Pastor Joby Martin

I grew up in Dillon, South Carolina. It's a town of about 5,000 people, and my daddy used to say, "The best thing to come out of Dillon is I-95." There's a very high probability that you've never heard of Dillon, but if you've ever driven on I-95 through South Carolina, you've been near Dillon when you drove past South of the Border, the giant gas station.

I remember riding my bike one day with my best friend, Joey Peele, to a fireworks store at the South of the Border area. To a seven-year-old boy, there is not a more magical place than a fireworks store, and by God's grace, for some reason, the fireworks that are illegal in all the other states are legal in South Carolina.

Joey and I walked around that shop in wonder. We eventually met the owner, an older man who had roughly three fingers left on each hand. Joey and I stood at the counter and pointed to one firework after firework and asked the owner, "What does that one do?"

His response was, "It goes up in the air and goes 'boom'." We'd point to another one and ask what it did. He said again, "It goes up in the air and goes 'boom'." Another one. "It goes up in the air and goes 'boom'."

Something had happened over the years. This guy had lost his awe. What was magical to us had become ordinary to him. I think that's a big problem with a lot of believers. We've lost our awe of God. We exchanged somewhere along the way the fact that the Creator of the Universe loves us and has called us into His global mission for just going to church sometimes. I think we need some help recovering a vision for all of life that is God-oriented and God-centered. That is exactly what my friend Matt has done in this book. He's stewarded everything that God has entrusted to Him to create this great resource to help you reorient your life to the glory of God.

You were made to do risky things. You were hardwired for hard. When God made you, He created you with incredible capacity and potential. You have the ability to live life abundantly. There are a few things that you need to know about yourself that will help you to live that abundant life.

First, your life was made by God for God. You have a purpose and a plan for your life. You are not just the accidental byproduct of a man loving a woman. When Matt and his company of engineers and designers create something, they have an intention and purpose for that thing. You were made by God, and the purpose for your life is to know and glorify God. There's a big problem, though. God created everything perfectly, but in the Garden of Eden, Adam and Eve, our original parents, rebelled against God's one rule and not only broke God's law but also broke God's heart and thereby brought sin into this world. And when sin entered, it brought with it all the brokenness that has saturated our world. We are all born separated from God because of their sin and our own.

Here's the greatest news in the world: God didn't leave us in our sin and brokenness; He sent His only Son, Jesus, to live the life we couldn't live and to die the death that we deserved. God honored Jesus' sacrifice as the payment for our sins so that if we would believe that what Jesus did counted for us, we would be forgiven and reconciled to Him. Everything about everything in your life can change because of what Jesus has done for us. That reconciliation to God by trusting in Christ is what enables you to live your life on purpose.

Second, everything in your life has been entrusted to you. God placed you where you were born, with the family that you were born into, with your personality and your giftings. He has given you everything; your job, your abilities, and the very breath in your lungs are all gifts from Him that have been entrusted to you not for you to consume, but for you to leverage for Him. You work hard at whatever job you have because God placed you there as His representative. You lead your family because He has entrusted them to you. You steward your time, talent, and treasures because they are all from Him and for Him. Again, knowing your purpose for your life leads to living your life in that vision and calling.

Third, your calling is not to comfort. You aren't just here to enjoy this life. You haven't been given the things in your life for your own amusement. You are a disciple who has been called to expand the glory of God to the ends of the earth by making disciples. Our sinful tendency is to make this life about us. That makes us use people to get things we love instead of using things to love people. That makes us consume instead of contributing. Life is about so much more than our comfort, which is why we take risks. We follow God into all that He has for us; comfort is not a Kingdom value. We leverage all that we have for His glory. We build churches. We send missionaries. We move to join Him in what He's doing. We start businesses and we carry the light of the gospel into dark places because that's what we were made to do and what we were called to do.

Fourth, we follow Him with joy. We don't lose the awe that the God of the universe would call us to join Him in His great global mission for His glory. Like the Psalmist says in

Psalm 2:8, we pray for the nations, the ends of the earth, to know Him. We take steps of faith and obedience to follow our Good Shepherd because He's worthy of it and because it brings us joy to be with Him and near Him. We draw near to Him because He promises that when we do that, He will draw near to us. We not only find our true meaning and purpose for our lives in Him but we also find true joy in Him alone.

So, my question to you is, what is He calling you to do? A mentor asked me years ago, what would you do, to the glory of God, if you knew it wouldn't fail? What would you do? Would you ask that girl to marry you? Would you go back to school? Would you start that company or a non-profit? Would you go on that mission trip? Would you give more, serve more, or lean in more? Why not do it today? What's holding you back? You were made to do risky things because God has called you to follow Him and to live for Him. Matt will help you do that if you'll lean into this book, and you'll take that next step of faith. In the words of William Borden, the millionaire who became a missionary, "no reserve, no retreats, no regrets." We give everything we have for the One who gave everything for us.

**Pastor Joby Martin**
Founder and Lead Pastor at The Church of Eleven22

# CHAPTER 1

# THE KINGDOM WAY

"WELL, MATT, THIS IS JUST HOW BUSINESS IS DONE."

As soon as I heard that, I pushed back from the table. I physically leaned back. They'd just put a generational wealth number in front of me. *This is just how business is done.* That may be. But it's not how *I* will do business. So I got up and walked away. The deal was over. Everything was over. I reset my company's revenue to zero, with zero clients.

At the time, I had seventeen full-time staff—and all seventeen supported me. They said in word and deed, "We don't know where you're going, Matthew, but we're going with you."

It was like *Jerry Maguire*—except it wasn't just one person. It was almost a dozen and a half; everyone left and came with me. Whatever I was doing, it had to be something right.

• • • •

What a book teaches matters. What matters more is *who* teaches it. That decides whether or not you can trust it. So before you read any further, you need to meet me first. Would you like to learn from the man you meet in the pages ahead? Read on, then decide if you can follow my advice. I can't promise that you will like what you read, but I can guarantee that you won't know what comes next.

I'm the son of an immigrant. My dad came to this country with nothing. His ancestors came to North America with nothing. I grew up in a solid, right-down-the-middle-class neighborhood. That was our lifestyle and everything that came with it. I have two brothers, including a twin, which was pretty rare back before IVF made them commonplace. Three sons to a home meant we were allowed to pick one activity—but all three had to agree what that would be. Mom wasn't doing multiple drop-offs or paying for multiple activities. So we didn't do karate or football like most kids did in the '90s because we could never all agree on either. So we ended up in middle school church-league basketball where we were the eighth-grade champions of Charlotte, North Carolina—still my greatest accomplishment in life.

When I got into high school, from day one, I was laser-focused on ROTC with the goal to join the Navy. During my last two years, I taught ROTC—two classes per semester—and achieved the rank of cadet commander for our Junior ROTC battalion. That earned me a nearly automatic bid into the Naval Academy and a Navy scholarship to Georgia Tech. I chose Georgia Tech because my great-uncle—the first Chinese-Jamaican immigrant in our family to come to the US—went there. I figured if I was going to be an engineer—then I'd follow in my great-uncle's footsteps and become a helluva engineer.

But that plan came undone after my first year at Georgia Tech. I was discharged from the Navy due to a sequester—they cut the size of the ROTC program, after cutting military bases. That changed everything. So, I did what any red-blooded southern boy might do: I joined a fraternity to party and skip physical fitness and ROTC drills.

Then 9/11 happened. And not long after, the Navy contacted me with an offer to re-enlist in ROTC and OCS and ultimately become an officer.

I didn't take it. I had already gone through the heartbreak of being forced out of the military after five years of preparation. At that point, I was deep into fraternity life and had decided to pursue a civilian engineering career.

As you might imagine, I had a *great* time at Georgia Tech. I was the poster boy for skipping class and pulling stunts, which I'll return to also shortly. Naturally, I wasn't the most focused student, but at a school like Tech, no one really went to class anyway. We were the Oregon Trail Generation—born between 1980 and 1984. We're fluent in both analog and digital. We were in college when Facebook first launched—back when there weren't even photos, thank goodness. (Half my fraternity brothers would go on to become prolific founders or senior executives at top Silicon Valley companies.)

As I tried to figure out my own career, I was advised that "design-build" was the future. That's where one company handles both engineering and construction. I wanted to stay in the South (you can't beat the year-round warm weather), so I took an opportunity with the original design-build company in America, based in Jacksonville, Florida: Haskell. They basically invented design-build way back in the 1960s.

I had an amazing ten-year career there. It completely

replaced what the Navy would've been for me. The old saying was "Join the Navy, see the world"—but instead of being deployed to the Persian Gulf or Afghanistan like so many of my own ROTC buddies who stayed in (or got back in) would, I got to travel the world a different way—by building factories.

Over that decade at Haskell, I racked up every professional certification or license I could, opened four foreign offices, and won three "International Project of the Year" awards. It was an absolute roller coaster of a ride. I learned a ton—everything from litigation (I sued the federal government on behalf of my employer and won a settlement, even after the feds claimed "sovereign immunity") to cutting-edge construction.

I built world-class facilities, including Haskell's first fully automated e-commerce fulfillment center as early as 2005. I led projects on the first driverless factory for Georgia-Pacific as well as the first carbon fiber aircraft manufacturing facilities. Eventually, I opened Haskell's offices in Kuala Lumpur, Shanghai, and Singapore. I also executed engineering projects in Europe, the Middle East, and Thailand.

At that point, I had climbed the proverbial mountain of employee accomplishment. What else was there? Well, nowadays, Elon Musk's companies have the colloquial nicknames, for example, "SpaceX University" and "Tesla University" because they're known for shaping young talent but not providing a long-term role in the business. That, too, was Haskell when I worked there. It was quietly assumed that my coworkers and I would eventually leave to start our own companies—either as niche competitors or in complementary engineering services. I eventually became part of that graduating class; I used to joke that I got a PhD in design-build before starting my own firm, Chang Robotics.

But I'm getting ahead of myself. Let's zoom in on my tenth year at Haskell. At the time, I was living in Shanghai. I was a licensed engineer there—the only foreign registered agent of a foreign-owned engineering or construction company in all of China. Then tragedy struck. Back home, one of my best friends—also my direct report—died suddenly while training for a triathlon. His name was Jared Bynum. We were both thirty years old. I was on a flight back to Shanghai, sitting on a plane in Atlanta, when we got the email. A group of us, all in shock, got off the plane. I don't think I had the maturity at the time to process it properly, but fortunately, my colleague (who's now the COO of the company) was on the flight with me.

"We need to get off," he said. "This is more important than the trip." So we grabbed our things, deboarded, and caught the very next flight back to Jacksonville.

I was close with Jared's widow and stayed with her and our friend group through the days leading up to the funeral. And that funeral was *massive*. It was held at a fairly large church in Jacksonville, but hundreds of people outside couldn't get in. That was the **first** time I came face-to-face with the idea of legacy. I asked myself, *How could my buddy—my direct report—have such a profound impact on so many people that he would overflow a church and fill a parking lot?*

I thought I knew Jared's story. His wife thought she knew his story. As it turned out, none of us had the *whole* story. Each of us had known a different version of Jared, and somehow, every person who knew him felt like they were uniquely part of his life.

At the funeral, a young, black kid from the projects came up to speak. Jared had been his big brother through the Big Brothers Big Sisters program. None of us—his wife included—

knew he had a little brother. The teenager shared that when mentors usually show up, they don't stick around. But Jared did. For a year straight, Jared just sat in silence with him during their mentoring time. At the start of the second year, the kid finally opened up and said, "You came back. No one's ever come back." And that began a deep relationship that lasted beyond the grave.

And that was Jared. He was an Ironman and marathoner. He was the lead bass guitarist in his church band—I didn't even know that. And of course he was a great husband. A fun guy. He loved to hang out and knew how to party. I knew him to be an excellent construction project manager that got important things done on time and on budget. Jared Bynum left behind a legacy that far exceeded his number of years on earth—through athletics, community service, faith, his professional work, and his marriage.

The night of the funeral, we held an impromptu after-party, sponsored by a local microbrewery Jared had frequented with all of us from Haskell. The only way we knew how to deal with our grief was to hang out and drink keg beer together.

We took that after-party back to Jacksonville Beach, to a friend's house. Being Georgia Tech guys, the only way we knew how to deal with intense emotions besides getting drunk was to burn things in the street. So we dragged all of a mutual friend's couches out into the middle of the road and lit them on fire—an effigy to him, right there in the street.

That's when a few of my buddies looked at me, sort of the leader of the after-party pack, and asked, "Hey Matt, what have you eaten today?"

"Nothing."

"Yeah, we should probably fix that. Things are going south fast." If you know what that means...

Anyway, we all walked (not drove) to the nearest place to eat: Mellow Mushroom Pizzeria in Jax Beach. We got a table and ordered some pizzas. One of my friends was newly married, and it happened to be Ladies Night—Thursday night at Jax Beach, a known spot for singles to meet.

We noticed the way he was eyeing all the women at the bar—his head practically spinning. In his whole life, he'd never been to a "Ladies Night," until now. (Jax Beach has the greatest ladies nights in the country, by the way.)

So I told my buddy, "Man, you really outkicked your coverage with your wife. But judging by the way your head's on a swivel, you may not be married much longer. Let's play a game. You point to a girl, and I'll invite her over for a slice of pizza. That way, you get the thrill of the hunt, but you didn't actually do anything wrong. You're completely indemnified with your wife. You can blame everything on me."

"Deal," he said.

"But you only get one. Choose wisely."

He surveyed the entire bar, thought carefully, and then pointed. "That one."

That one . . . is now my wife. At the time of this writing, we just had our fourth child. And when I walked up to her that night at the bar, she told me she wasn't very interested in pizza that late at night; but that she would go surfing with me. Meeting her, I risked it on the ultimate pick-up line (that has a 0.01% chance of working), "Hey, do you run marathons?" Turns out she did and those strong legs almost buckled upon hearing the magic phrase.

After that night, I lost all interest in returning to Shanghai. I did go back and continue to work for Haskell. In China, I wrapped up a few assignments and told my supervisor shortly afterwards, in effect, "Look, I'm done with China. I gave you three years. We got it off the ground, but I think I'm ready to move on."

"That's great!" he said. "You'd actually make an excellent executive at this company, after all your world conquest and successful projects."

"Exactly what I was hoping you'd say," I said. This was cool; I'd get the anticipated thrill of leading a company, but the comfort and predictability that comes with *not* having to start your own, like so many ex-Haskell guys did.

So he continued. "Yeah, in about ten years, we'll promote you to an executive. In the meantime, here's your desk, and here are the reports you need to do. Just keep doing those until it's your turn."

Oh.

Ten years.

Oh.

Look, I'm one of the first millennials. We don't do "until it's your turn." So I started looking around. Right away, I got two job offers. The first was from Amazon; they offered me the Director of Capital role (in 2014). I thought, *Selling stuff online? That sounds promising. This whole e-commerce thing might have legs.*

I flew out to Seattle for the interview. I'd spent time on the Google campus before then, previously visiting the campus with some of my very highly-paid Georgia Tech friends who were managers there. We rode the colorful bicycles and worked out at all the crazy fitness amenities (it's just like the movies, by the way.) Anyway, I had expectations of what innovation energy should feel like. But Amazon was the opposite. When I arrived, they asked if I wanted lunch brought in. I said, "No,

I'd rather check out the café." So I went to the corporate café and saw sad people with headphones on, all staring at their phones and eating alone. I'll never forget—I ordered a tilapia quinoa bowl for $17. *I'm going to be out $17 every day for lunch? Every day?*

At Google, food was free. At Amazon, everything felt transactional (it was.)

I tried to sit down with one group.

"Hey guys, mind if I join you? I'm interviewing here."

They moved their trays a bit, and one said, "This is a private conversation."

So I tried another group—same thing. Everyone looked at me with suspicion, like I was intruding. I thought, *This is not a culture worth relocating to cold, rainy Seattle for.*

The second offer I got was from one of the country's oldest construction firms—founded around 1855. They wanted to launch a company to compete with Haskell.

The interviewer asked me, "Can you start an engineering business for us, so we can offer both engineering and construction?"

*Now this is more my speed. Exciting.* I wouldn't just be building the same e-commerce thing over and over again.

Oh, here's a quick footnote: An old Georgia Tech classmate got that Amazon director job instead and now runs Amazon's global robotics program. It probably would've been a great path for either of us—it worked out very well for him.

The engineering business worked better for me. I accepted and moved to their base in Des Moines, Iowa, where I lived through the entire 2015 and 2016 primary then general election cycle. What an amazing place to be—every politician came through, making their case in every single county, and I was in the mix for all of it. That's why I was one of the first to support Donald Trump for president. Not because of his politics, but because of the change he represented. We needed to shake the box—that was my personality having moved on from Haskell after a decade to build an in-house startup company. I saw Trump's grassroots, working class support flourish firsthand. My projects took me through rural Pennsylvania and rural Minnesota in particular. I'd see farmers putting up forty-foot-wide Trump flags on homemade billboards. That passion was real, and I have never seen anything like it before or since.

Meanwhile during the campaign, we won five international customers in our first year and a half. That's rare in engineering—it's a high-trust industry, and new clients don't come easy. But we were setting the landscape on fire with our success.

I built the entire team and opened the company's first Jacksonville office, which ended up being the most diverse office in the whole company. More than half of the African-Americans in that hundred-year-old company worked in my office. We had women, Asians, black engineers—doing world-class design and engineering together. Not because I hired based on "woke" values to signal "inclusiveness" for its own sake, but because I looked for the best—and knew how to find it just about anywhere and everywhere.

But just when we thought we were killing it—and wondering how we'd even find enough people to hire for all the work we had—the HR lady from Iowa showed up on a Monday morning. Every company has "that HR lady," and everyone knows what her unexpected presence means.

*Uh-oh. She took the 5:30 AM out of Des Moines. She's here before lunch in Jacksonville. This is bad.*

The moment she walked in and saw our design team through the conference room windows—wearing Hawaiian shirts and flip-flops, gathered around a table looking at plans like something out of a stock photo—I just blurted out, "Team, go to your offices and save your work. Right now. Go."

"Matt, can you gather everyone back here in the conference room?" she asked after everyone had hurried off.

"Sure. Give us ten minutes."

We all went in, and she started handing out folders. Inside, a card with a 1-800 number. And every question we asked—*What's going on? Why is this happening?*—got the same answer:

"It's in the folder. Call the number."

That was it. The entire office was shut down that day. And not just ours. The Houston and Kansas City offices were shut down, too. It was all part of a cost-saving move by a new CEO. He looked at the books and basically asked his henchmen, "What are the newest offices? What are the most expensive offices?"—and axed them.

Jacksonville came up on both lists—the newest office *and* one of the most expensive—so we were gone. Houston and Kansas City, too.

I'd just been fired and was a few weeks away from graduating from Jacksonville University with my executive master's, which I'd been working on in evenings and weekends alongside enjoying quality time with my wife (the hottie my friend picked out in Jax Beach.) So I went home that day at lunch, and my wife thought I was joking when I told her about the HR lady and the phone number on the card. Never mind that I didn't have my company truck anymore as of that morning. They took that on my way out, too. Me being new to marriage, I expected some sympathy and a back rub. My wife thought I was pranking her (perhaps I had a history of doing so, but that's for another chapter, maybe even another book.)

Anyway, the next morning, I got up and found her making blueberry pancakes.

"What are you doing?"

"Making pancakes."

"Why? You never make pancakes."

"Oh, to be supportive of you," she said. "I'm so sorry."

"Well, that was *yesterday*. I'm not sad anymore," I said. "Today's for getting to work."

"You've always wanted to start your own company. Maybe now's the time."

Later that week, I was with the middle school boys church, where I volunteered as their student leader. We were teaching a lesson on covenants. Everyone wrote a covenant on an index card. Theirs were very seventh-grade: *I won't kick my sister, I'll clean up my room, I'll listen to my parents.* I wrote, *Dear God, I will start a Christian engineering company.*

Then we did what you do on Covenant Night—we placed our cards on the altar. And we assumed the Holy Spirit extracted those and uploaded them into some kind of Web3 database for permanent record. But you don't really know where it goes. Still, I felt—and still feel—bound to that covenant.

A week later, I got a call from a former client in Iowa.

"Matt, what are you doing?"

"Sitting on the couch in my pajamas, drinking coffee, working on my laptop—well, my wife's laptop. I don't have mine anymore, and I can't afford a new one."

"Well, I want you in Iowa on Monday. But before you get here, start a company, get a suit, and get a haircut."

I did two out of the three; just google me to see my hair.

I showed up in Iowa that Monday, spent the week working inside a manufacturing plant, coaching on performance and automation. At the end of the week, my former client walked me into the Accounts Payable office and said, "Matt, this is our AP clerk. AP clerk, this is Matt. Get him paid. He's got a company."

Exactly one week after Covenant Night, we had our first paying customer. We were in business.

The same week, I showed up to my group meeting for our capstone project at Jacksonville University. Everyone was surprised to see me—I was usually on a plane twice a week and rarely around for midweek meetings.

"What are you doing here?"

"I'm here to do the project. And by the way, we're going to deliver the greatest capstone project in the history of JU's executive MBA. So let's get to work."

"What's with the change?"

"Well . . . I just got fired."

One of the CEOs in my group let out a deep belly laugh—he couldn't stop.

I said, "This really isn't funny."

Meanwhile, one of our classmates—a grandmother getting her executive master's—came around and started giving me that back rub I deserved, telling me it's going to be OK.

I looked over at the CEO and said, "*She's* doing what *you're* supposed to be doing. I need sympathy here!"

He said, "This is so good for me. And it's going to be great for you, too."

That moment led directly to what is now the federal government-sponsored autonomous mass transit project—my second client became the US Department of Transportation and the Jacksonville Transportation Authority. They needed someone to envision and engineer a fully autonomous mass transit system—and they hired me to do it.

And those two gigs got my newborn company, Chang Robotics, off the ground.

We've had some very near-misses along the way. One example, we were the runner-up to design and build Starbucks' Shanghai Roastery—the only one of their roasteries located outside the U.S. All their global coffee otherwise comes from America. Their most iconic is in York, Pennsylvania. Shanghai was the first roastery on foreign soil.

But losing that job turned out to be a blessing. The construction of that project—the Shanghai Roastery—hit its midpoint during the COVID-19 lockdown. The crews on site were confined to the construction zone and forced to live in shipping containers, finishing the work without being allowed to visit their families. They were, for all intents and purposes, jailed on-site for nearly two years. There's a very real chance that me, my team, or some portion of us would've been in those containers, finishing that project under lockdown. So what a blessing to come in second place. I feel for the other guys though.

We've also had a host of successes. Most of my business expansion has come through mentorship—we even wrote a full chapter about that in the book. Mentors taught me new dimensions of business and new ways to think about growth.

Now, our company history breaks into two "chapters". In the first chapter, we focused solely on engineering and robotic implementation. From 2017 to 2021, we delivered some of the most advanced projects in the world. We built the largest coffee roastery in the world in Spartanburg, South Carolina—trading one coffee project for another, this one for Keurig. We deployed the largest system of autonomous robots on Earth. For Wayfair, we designed the first fully automated e-commerce facility for non-conveyables. And we designed America's first robotic pharmacy, for Walgreens. All of those were full design-and-build projects. That four-year stretch was a high-flying period. We built an incredible systems integration company—one that caught the entire industry off guard. We were the insurgents, not bound by the legacy methods of companies that had been doing things the same way for twenty or thirty years. We started fresh—and we moved fast.

Four years into the venture, we were effectively raided by private equity. They had to have us—and they got us. There were six company owners in the venture. Five out of the six sold to private equity. All it took was putting a big number in front of them. And they were in. The only one who didn't go in? Yours truly.

That was after I had personally led the strategy for forming the deal and making the sales pitch to the private equity firm. At the time, I was too pollyannaish to realize—they weren't investing *in* us. They were buying the companies. They were buying *the people*.

It had been framed to me as, "These folks are interested in investing in *us*." But once I saw the culture and business principles driving the deal, I realized the business principles were effectively zero. It was:

- Step 1: Make more money for us.
- Step 2: If you're confused, return to Step 1.

The culture was completely antithetical to what I believe

in. At one point, during the deal process, they circulated a list of all employees—and assigned a dollar value next to each person's name. That's when I turned against the deal.

I asked, "Are we selling employees?"

They said, "Oh no, no, this is just how investment deals work."

I said, "But it *looks* like we're selling employees. We're literally putting a price tag next to every person's name. And after this deal, they'll work for a different company—without having had a say in the matter."

"Well, Matt, this is just how business is done."

You know what happened next. I pushed back, said no, and *Jerry Maguire*'d out of there. Whatever I was doing, I was doing something right—and the people around me saw it, too.

During the separation process, which involved about two months of intense litigation, my constant prayer was simple: *Dear God, let me act like Jesus, and let You be glorified through how I respond in this situation.*

That might sound like an impossible prayer when you've got lawyers bearing down on you, when everything feels adversarial and transactional. It doesn't seem like the legal system—or back-and-forth attorney letters—would be a place to glorify Jesus. But the outcome showed me that I at least got it *mostly* right. That's why I talk about glorifying God and living like Jesus during hard times—because I got to live it.

The second "chapter" of Chang Robotics—these last four years, from 2021 to today, the time of this writing—has been the most financially challenging period we've ever had. We were reset to zero. And at that point, we had a lot more mouths to feed.

We had to figure it out—fast. And that meant leaning hard

on divine intervention. My daily prayer during that phase of the company was: *God, You're sovereign over everything. The whole world spins in Your hands. You tilt the earth on its axis. If You want us to be successful, we will be. If You want it to be over, it will be. We submit. Just tell us what You want us to do, and we'll design it and build it—whatever it is.*

Then, out of nowhere, we got a call from Coca-Cola in Taiwan.

"We're building a new manufacturing center to serve the entire nation of Taiwan. Right now, we import most of our products from China. But we need to cut off that supply line. We need to be self-sufficient."

The challenge? They wanted to build a 100-acre manufacturing operation on just ten acres—right in downtown Taipei. And the facility had to deliver beverages daily to every corner store in the city. That's a whole lot of manufacturing and logistics to squeeze onto a ten-acre footprint.

We leaned on the experience we'd gained while developing a vertical manufacturing plant for PepsiCo in Singapore. Using that foundation, we designed for Coca-Cola a seven-story manufacturing center that produces all the products they need for the Taiwan market. That one phone call—and that one engagement—saved the company.

For about six months, Coca-Cola Taiwan was our only client. But from there, we slowly and steadily rebuilt our client base. Today, we hold master service agreements with multiple Fortune 500 manufacturing companies.

Consider that early in our company relaunch, I had lost all of my partners. At the time of the private equity exit, I had been a distributor for some of the world's top robotics and automation brands. But I lost all of those distribution rights—along with our client contracts.

A year into flying solo, I was scratching and clawing, practically begging companies to partner with us. But this past year alone, I've had two Fortune 1000 international robotics companies slide into my LinkedIn DMs and *beg* me to partner with them. Things have definitely turned around. These days, people come to *us*. I don't have to sell anything. I evaluate proposals, nitpick them, and decide if I want to accept the deal. It's a very different position from where we started.

I call 2024 "The Year of Awards." We were the only company named to both *Inc.* Magazine's "Top Companies" list and *Fast Company*'s "Most Innovative Firms" list. That's also why I now write for both publications—they recruited me as a technical contributor after the awards.

We're recognized because we recognize what matters most. I spent two years designing Jacksonville's autonomous mass transit system. Then I served Jacksonville University, helping to build out their STEAM Institute. (STEAM stands for—Science, Technology, Engineering, Arts, and Math, by the way.)

About a year and a half ago, I was called into service again—this time to build the Innovation Hub for the City of Jacksonville. That includes recruiting Florida State University's engineering and research college to relocate to Jacksonville (as well as FAMU, Florida's leading historically black university.) It also means getting all of our major civic and private institutions aligned around one initiative: building an innovation economy in Jacksonville.

As of today, we're a finalist in the national competition to become the National Science Foundation's next Innovation Hub. That designation comes with a significant financial purse. We're pouring into the city.

Honestly, I give more time than I probably should—to the city, to my alma mater at Jacksonville University, and to our largest local healthcare foundation. We're working to expand access to primary care for rural and indigent populations. I also serve on the board of Lifework Leadership, the premier Christian leadership organization, helping them find ways to translate biblical principles into real-world business practices.

Alongside the company story, I've had four kids and built five houses. It's been, in a word, *busy*. I'm also a "Bitcoin maximalist," or maxi for short—I've been in it since 2014. I used to bring people into my office and teach them how to buy Bitcoin. And nobody ever did. At the time, it probably seemed expensive—just magic internet money. But now, people say, "Wait; didn't he try to show me this over a decade ago?"

Let's just say I have a very unusual risk tolerance by most people's standards. But it comes from a biblical worldview: *Nothing is yours. You're just a steward.*

The parable of the talents inspires everything I do. We're commanded to take what we're given and *wager it all* for the Master's glory. Everything I have—my opportunities, my energy, my skills—are gifts. Even the good genetics. All four of my children bear the mark of Genghis Khan. How could they fail? I come from a great family and historical lineage. My parents are still married—and honestly, I think that's the greatest gift anyone can have in America, married parents.

I have a wonderful wife and four healthy, thriving kids. We live in a great place, we have a great lifestyle, and I try to surround myself with people who come from very little but have that hunger to rise. That's who I'm drawn to.

In this book, we'll talk about guys like Dr. Nahshon Nicks. His father is currently in prison at Attica; his mother passed away from a fentanyl overdose. And yet he's out there doing the Lord's work every single day—boldly. That gets us up to the present day.

So what's the future? Well, during all this, we also started five companies. I don't process it that way, but if you're a banker or a lawyer, you'd say: "Matt Chang owns five companies." And we're still expanding. Since 2022, we've deferred all dividends—which, understandably, probably irritates some of my shareholders. But my shareholders are also my employees. We're employee-owned. And we've poured 100 percent of our excess into building new ideas, new companies, and placing the bets we believe in.

The funny thing is, I get *very* excited about tariffs, elections, reshoring, currency shifts—all of it. Because every single thing happening in the country right now is validating decisions we made years ago.

Do I think I'm that wise—that I predicted all this? Absolutely not. I don't fully understand how global markets work. But I do believe those decisions were inspired by prayer. *God, tell us what to do. We'll design it and build it.*

Whenever I find myself in impossible situations—where I can't even find an outside counselor to help me get perspective—I go back to one prayer. I call it the "Open Doors and Closed Doors" prayer. I picture it like standing in the hallway of a Marriott or a Hampton Inn. All you can see in both directions are identical doors stretching endlessly. And my prayer is always: *Dear God, fasten tight the doors that aren't meant for me. No matter how badly I want in, don't let me through. But for the doors You've opened for me, let them swing wide before I even get there—and grant me the boldness to step inside. Once I'm in, give me the clarity and strength to handle what's inside.*

If God grants me that—just that—I believe, through the maturity and training I've received, I can handle the rest.

So where are we today? We are the global patent holder for the only safe alternative to PFAS in food packaging, i.e., plastic crap nobody should be putting in their bodies. How did *that* happen? That was before I even knew who Robert F. Kennedy, Jr. and the Make America Healthy Again ("MAHA") movement were. And we were already investing in the space to . . . make America healthy again. God is in it.

You see, part of being a risk-taker means meeting *the future in the present*. It means getting there first. Being willing to look foolish to the skeptics and the safety-players of today.

And then—when they eventually show up in the future, where you've already been for months or years—they may hand-wave it all away and act like it was obvious the whole time. "We all saw it coming."

The truth is, I did what hadn't been done. I did what didn't always make sense at the time. I took the risk; I moved in boldness. And that sense of courage—that *gusto*—I pray is contagious to you, reading this book. It might be exactly what you're looking for. I hope and assume it is.

Courage is what makes it possible to take risks—to take shareholder money and invest it in something as weird-sounding as "magic invisible paper science." Yes, we've placed some big bets. That's also why I don't lose sleep signing banking documents to get us levered up for mega projects. You've got to take bold action.

If you hand me a hundred-million-dollar project, I can't afford that project—not up front. Because I have to buy everything for it before I ever see a single check from you. That's the reality. Now, if you're a Fortune 1,000 company, you're fine with that arrangement. But the reason I'm not afraid to sign those bank documents? It's because half of my "assets" are things the banks don't even consider to be real, but I do, which means they can't take it from me. Even if they take my house, I'll be walking out the front door with magic internet money and houses on foreign surfing beaches—and I'll be just fine.

But it runs deeper than that. Everything I have—100 percent of it—was given to me by God. The good and the bad. And if He decides to take it all away, that's His call. He can do it, no matter how diversified I am, how wise my financial choices seem, or how I present myself publicly. He could take it in a heartbeat—literally—if I no longer had a heartbeat or breath. We're all confronted with that reality. So if God gave me what I have, my job is to make the most of it while I have it—for the glory of the Master. And if He wants me to have more, I trust He'll give more. The only thing we can take to Heaven is more people. All the money, houses, and cars . . . stay here when we're gone, and other people will use it or take it to Goodwill.

One thing I often say when people ask about being financially biblical—because that's the number one question that comes up—is this: *God is good at math.* Look, He invented DNA. He hung the planets in orbit. I think He knows what He's doing. So if there are two businesses . . .

One that tithes faithfully from its revenue—giving back to the Kingdom first. And another that occasionally does good things, like sponsoring a kid's softball league when there's leftover cash . . .

Which business do you think God's going to bless? The one that's generous *first*? Or the one that only gives when it "feels right"?

"You can't tithe from the business," the lawyers and experts told me. Why not? "Well, you don't know what the next quarter holds. You could have an operating loss, your clients might not pay, you need to preserve cash flow . . ."

All of those things have happened to us. But none of them change our obedience in the moment. Because we are called to give our *first* and our *best*. That's what makes it worship. And yet you'll be hard-pressed to find a Christian financial advisor who will tell you to be generous *from your business*. They just don't exist. But we're doing it, and it's working out great.

Here's how I think about it: **10 percent is nothing.** Now, to Ray Dalio or the guy who runs BlackRock, 10 percent is a *lot*. If you return 10 percent in a year, you're in the top quartile. You've beat the market. But we're striving for *multiples*. And in a multiplication economy, 10 percent is a rounding error. If God is pouring favor on you, if you're multiplying, you won't even miss it. The 10 percent that the finance guys were so afraid to part with? You won't even notice it's gone.

So yes, I want people like **you**—those who *have means*, and those *who will have means* because of the risks they're taking—to be financially obedient *from day one*. The world is full of great nonprofits. They're all struggling for funding. One of the easiest, most impactful things you can do as an entrepreneur is *make money* and *support them*. When you do that, your labor in the marketplace gets amplified by people who wake up every day to serve their communities and make lives better.

I firmly believe this: If you believe in Jesus and you call Him Lord and Savior, then you'll run your company *that* way. I have a story for every business challenge you can name. Trust me—I've been there. Been through it. Got the scar tissue to prove it. And yes, I'm still here. Including betrayal, even. I've been burned - badly. And I've met hundreds of founders, leaders, and investors who've gone through the same. Embezzlement. Stolen intellectual property. A partner who made off with the business. People you trusted—people you believed in—who stabbed you in the back. It's one of the most common, least talked-about reasons why people stop risking, stop giving, stop betting on others. And I get it. It's frustrating, and it's traumatic.

But here's what I believe: Betrayal should make you wiser, not smaller. You can be smarter about how you structure deals, protect assets, and vet people—but you don't have to become someone who stops trusting altogether. That's not strength. That's fear dressed up like wisdom. And we don't build Kingdom impact—or generational wealth—by living in fear. We do it by risk. Because risk-taking is Biblical.

• • • •

Your success will have an eternal impact. You can follow biblical principles to launch a Kingdom-building changing business or enterprise or ministry or charity. That said, is the way this book teaches all this right for you? Let me ask you: Do you want to learn all **this**?

- You want to transform your business but are afraid of how to start.
- You have failed in the past and are not confident you can do it again and be successful, but you sure want to.
- You want to know how to be wise and leverage the teachings of the Bible for your leadership role.

- You're looking for best practices on business strategy and decision-making.
- You'd like to surround yourself with wise, Christ-loving advisors.
- You want practical, immediately applicable tools and tips to jumpstart your business and ministry.

We have the Bible and business books and also sermons, of course, and yet none of the above seems obvious. It seems more like a secret. Did you know that 67 percent of new businesses never make it to ten years? The stats can be even worse for non-profits; only 0.4 percent of businesses ever reach $10 million in revenue. Christians seeking to take risks and build enterprises for the Kingdom feel like they are left with two choices: Either go with charity and follow the poverty gospel, or follow the dog-eat-dog way of the world in business. I'm here to tell you that you can build a successful enterprise *and* do it God's way. Using the principles taught in the Bible can dramatically increase your odds. Most fail, so do what they don't; do the opposite of what they do. And most are playing it safe, which is unbiblical. The Bible encourages risk-taking, and includes instructions and inspiration. However, we are never taught to read the Bible to help us take the risk necessary to build for the Kingdom. And so I'm going to equip you with guidance and strategy to make best use of this timeless tool, the Bible. Here's what we're going to cover how to:

- Accept your calling before launching your mission.
- Start small but think Kingdom-sized.
- Discern God's calling through study, prayer, and service.

- Lead before you're in charge.
- Build a vision worth following.
- Make radical risk feel like biblical obedience.
- Confront betrayal without losing your heart.
- Multiply impact through mentorship.
- Tithe from your first invoice, not your last dollar.
- Create a generosity-powered company culture.
- Think like a steward, not a hoarder.
- Develop Kingdom-level financial literacy.
- Push through lawsuits, pivots, and debt with spiritual integrity.
- Invest in people like you'd want someone to invest in you.
- Network without being needy.
- Become the mentor you wish you had.
- Find courage through covenant.
- Design and build when the world feels uncertain.
- Avoid reputation-risk paralysis.
- Wager it all for the Master—and win more than you ever imagined possible.

If any of that excites you, and you believe that I know what I'm talking about—and trust that I **will** talk about all of it— then let's carry on. Read on.

# CHAPTER 2

# THE STATE OF PREPARATION

**D****ID YOU KNOW? THE AVERAGE AGE OF A** successful company founder is forty-five. Do you know why? Well, you could probably list off a half-dozen reasons, all of which make sense. And yet there is one catch-all reason: **You're prepared**. By that age, you have a publicly available track record. And that record is one of <u>trust</u>. You have demonstrated that you are trustworthy before now asking others to trust you. And that includes trusting yourself. You've been through enough to know what you need to know, and you're also aware of what you *don't*; you have far fewer "unknown unknowns." So when you take risks, you're doing it with better judgment. You make smarter decisions, you invest more wisely, and you move with discernment.

Before a vacationer jumps off a paradise waterfall cliff into the crisp waters below, what do they do? They toss a rock down first. Or they wade in from the shallows. Or they climb down to look around before they leap. Risk-takers who survive and thrive did their homework first. It's starting small before jumping big.

If you peeped the table of contents before reading this book, you might recall the sequence of the book; here, we're preparing to start small. We're in the early phase of building experience—what I call **career currency**. That's a simpler way of describing "the 10,000-hour rule." It takes 10,000 hours to master something, they say. And your first skill really does take 10,000 hours. A university education, for example, is about 10,000 hours. Your first skill is expensive in terms of time and effort. But then your goal becomes talent stacking, as bestselling author Scott Adams puts it—building one new skill on top of another. Each of these additional skills gets faster to learn. In my current career stage, it takes me about 500 hours to pick up a new skill, which is quite efficient.

We want our future leaders and risk-takers to be diligent in serving others—not just working, but *serving*—and that means stacking as many skills as possible. That's the stage of preparation, and we're in it making the most of it before we lead, before we take a massive risk. This is why, by the way, I firmly believe young people should not launch startups straight out of college. Big companies offer training and exposure—the perfect place to talent-stack. Here, there are world-class clients, world-class projects, and world-class problems, all in a structure that prevents you from wasting time on having to figure everything out yourself. You can just focus on doing your part on a great team. That's a luxury you don't get when you're on your own.

Now, I do love to dunk on companies like Deloitte and McKinsey—they're my two favorite punching bags—but they are still excellent places to start your career. If you land at McKinsey, your very first consulting project might be for Coca-Cola. Wow. Yes, really. The biggest cola company in the world will ask *you* for advice. And also, you'll get to travel. A lot. To amazing places. You'll be surrounded by smart people. You'll learn how to operate in the business world at a high level.

That's what the state of preparation looks like—demonstrating your trustworthiness, stacking your talents, and doing it on someone else's dime. All by proving that you can be a fantastic employee. "Whoever can be trusted with little can also be trusted with much." And during that trust-proving time, you should earn raises, promotions, and increasing responsibility. These are the signals that you're in the right phase, doing it right.

The productive mindset for the state of preparation is, very simply, *Never say no.* For young people entering the workforce, your mental rule should be to say yes to every opportunity. Because when you say yes, you get exposed to new things. And that exposure is what allows you to continue stacking talents.

Now, let's take a quick detour on that subject. Because the most common explanation of talent stacking—outside of Scott Adams' material including the worldwide bestsellers *Reframe Your Brain* and *How to Fail at Almost Everything and Still Win Big*—is actually wrong. Or, at the very least, so uninformed that it's useless. The flawed, non-Adams version of talent stacking goes something like this:

> If I learn a bunch of different things, that's talent stacking.

No. Wrong. I'll explain why. The original concept of a "stack" reminds us of the phrase "full-stack developer."

And what is a full-stack developer? It's someone who can do everything necessary to roll out a complete digital product—whether it's an app, a website, or a database-driven tool used by businesses or consumers. A full-stack developer handles it all:

- The design and initial wireframes
- The coding
- The build
- The QA testing
- The monitoring
- The debugging
- The API integrations
- . . . everything.

But here's the key: All skills are adjacent. All of their knowledge bases are interrelated and compound one another.

The version of talent stacking that's floated around in mainstream career advice is more like, "Well, if you know C++, you should learn to play the guitar." Or, "If you're a creative person, go learn accounting to balance it out." That's not a stack. That's just being well-rounded, which may or may not do much for your career or your success in a future venture. Scott Adams' original idea of talent stacking is that each skill multiplies the others—not adds to them—because they're connected. They build on each other.

Here's another example. Let's say you're a strong writer. You can write powerful, persuasive content. Now, what should you do? You should learn how to deliver that writing through video. Show your face on camera. Learn how to read a script, speak confidently, memorize, and present.

But that's not all—you now also need to learn:

- Fashion and personal presentation
- Video editing
- Lighting
- Social media distribution
- What makes something go viral
- Marketing strategy
- Sound design, music selection, clips, and a whole lot more

Every piece that amplifies your written word through another medium becomes part of the stack.

Let's take another example to land the point home (and give you useful ideas for building your own talent stack.) Say you have a flair for making homemade pastries. You're one of those bread people. You're great at it. Now, should you go get a business administration degree?

Maybe. Maybe not. Depends on what you want to do. If your dream is to franchise a bakery, then yes, you'll probably want to learn business. But what's the first step? Before you get the degree—go work in a bakery. If you're twenty-four, and you've had a few jobs but breadmaking is your passion—you feel like it's what you're meant to do—don't just quit everything and jump. Don't risk it all without learning first.

*Before you leap, look.*

Let's wrap the bakery example—then I'll relate it to my own career. You see, it's one thing to be able to bake bread at home. It's another thing entirely to bake using commercial kitchen equipment. And then it's yet another level to package that bread in a way customers want to buy it in a retail setting.

You have to handle customer service, run point-of-sale systems, and order your ingredients—not from Publix, but from restaurant supply chains. Then there's managing inventory with a mix of durable and perishable goods. That's a whole different world. So the real progression from "I'm great at baking" becomes:

- Can I run a commercial kitchen?
- Can I manage the logistics of a retail operation?
- Can I train others to do it, so I'm not the one mixing and kneading dough every day?

In my own career, that evolution looked like this:

I started with engineering, then moved into project management, and then into construction supervision. Those were my core three. And each one is a full profession on its own—each with a certifying authority: the Board of Professional Engineers, the Project Management Institute, OSHA, and so on.

Once I had that foundation, I added the skill that made me the most uncomfortable: business development and sales. That was the big leap. Still adjacent, but a very different discipline. One is doing; the other is persuading.

Once I stacked those four—engineering, project management, construction supervision, and business development—that's when things really started to take off. Then came accounting and finance. And from there, the stack keeps growing.

What is often done instead, especially in nonprofits and ministry, is, let's say, competence at a level two or three, but dreams are level 100. The numbering scale we're using doesn't really matter because you get the gist; when someone experiences a little success—let's say they've been leading a men's Bible study for a year—they start thinking, *I should plant a church!* And yet they have no sense of what level fifteen looks like. Or level forty. Or even level five. They don't know what the path between here and there looks like.

In the nonprofit world, the biggest skill gap that all future leaders will need is **fundraising**. You launch a nonprofit because you're a doer. You're doing ministry. People are praising your work, your heart, your impact. But the moment you start leading the organization, you're responsible for funding it. Most people aren't ready for that. It's the same jump I made from "being good at my job" to "selling the company's services." From doing ministry to fundraising for it. That gap is *huge*.

You might have all the other skills—doctrine, seminary education, people skills, empathy—but now you need to learn the most uncomfortable thing: Ask people for money. Not as a passive hope, wish, or even prayer, but as an intentional, strategic aspect of leadership.

For many nonprofit founders, that's a new muscle. In their past roles, fundraising was handled by someone else. Or there was a church budget. Or a faithful donor. But now they're the one responsible for keeping the lights on. It's kind of terrifying.

What helps bridge that gap? The very same things we talked about earlier:

- Presentation skills
- Writing and scripting
- Social media and messaging
- Personal branding
- Visuals, style, confidence

I've seen this firsthand. I've trained the most prolific fundraiser in Jacksonville, Florida: Ron Armstrong. Ron launched a ministry called Sponsored by Grace. It's like Compassion International, but for kids in Jacksonville. Instead of sponsoring a child overseas, Christians in Florida can sponsor a local child in need.

Now, when I met him, Ron was doing this part-time—Saturdays, Sundays, just "bopping along." But I invested in him. I believed in what he was building and saw him committed to a state of preparation. Once he developed that next layer of skills, he took off. Let me tell you how that went.

Early in my mentorship with Ron, I asked him, "What's the number that would make you quit your full-time job so you could do the ministry full-time?"

He'd already seen success doing the ministry part-time, and I saw that he had the potential to make the leap into real leadership.

He thought about it and said, "My family needs $3,000 a month, minimum, to survive."

His wife had some income, too—she worked at a church and probably brought in around $3,000 a month on her own.

Then I asked, "How many months would you need to get traction?"

"I'd need five."

So right there in the meeting, I handed him a $15,000 check.

He looked at me and said, "I guess I'm quitting my job tomorrow."

"Great. That's a great place to start."

I then enrolled him in a one-year mentorship program through a nonprofit I run called Tentmakers. We pair three business owners with one mentee each per year. That was

Ron's next step.

We started taking him through the business basics.

First question: "Do you have insurance?"

"No. Why would I need that?"

I said, "Because you're working with children. That's a lawsuit waiting to happen. Let's fix that now."

We talked about policies and procedures. As much as I hate bureaucracy, it's essential, especially when you're sending care workers into children's homes alone. You need guidelines in place. "Be wise as serpents, innocent as doves."

Then he came to me with his first fundraising pitch. Inspired by what he was doing for underprivileged children in the community, a local business owner had asked Ron, "How can I help?"

Now, what I had to teach Ron is this: *When a wealthy person says "How can I help?", what they're really asking is, "How much money do you need?"* But they don't want to say it that way—so you have to know how to interpret it.

I told him, "Don't speak to this man until you bring me your draft pitch first."

So he did.

Here was his pitch:

> Mr. Business Owner, I'd like you to personally volunteer every Saturday in my poor communities, because I need you to be invested in the community. And I'd also like to offer you the opportunity to sign up for the Gold Sponsorship Package, which gets your name on the back of our 5K t-shirt—for just $3,000 a year.

I let him get all the way through the pitch.

Then I said, "Get up. You're fired. That was the worst I've ever seen."

So he stood up, a little shocked and not 100 percent sure if I was serious, and stepped away from the table.

"OK, stop. Now, come back here and sit down. Let's try again." I paused once he followed. "Look, first off, I'm a business owner. I'm growing my business. I've got my own employees to worry about. I have kids at home. My wife already complains I don't have enough time on the weekends. So this requirement to serve every Saturday? That's a nonstarter. That's an encumbrance to partnership. You're blocking the ideal relationship with this donor. Do you even need volunteers right now?"

"No. We have a ton of volunteers."

"Then why are you asking the rich man to volunteer? He's going to be a terrible one. He'll show up half the time, cancel the rest, and constantly send you excuses from a vacation or a business trip. Second, do you actually believe he wants his name on the back of a cheap, made-in-China 5K t-shirt?"

"Well, I don't know . . . it's the best thing I can offer."

"No, it's not. That's not an offer. That's insulting. You've clearly never seen money or interacted with people who have it." So I gave him a new strategy. "Tell him five stories. Real stories. Show him life change."

"Here's a child headed down a terrible path—now look at where they are after getting involved with Sponsored by Grace. Here's a teenager who lost their father to gang violence and had given up on life. Here's a high school student on track to drop out—who now has a diploma, a job, and a future. Show the outcomes. Show what Grace did. And finally—tell your story. What led you to this work? What was your call to action? What experience in your life broke your heart and called you to build this ministry?"

Ron himself has an incredible testimony. He grew up in seven different foster homes before graduating high school. After that, his profession—his identity—became narco trafficking. That's what he did before he met Jesus.

"That's the story you need to tell," I told him. "Sit across from this business owner and tell him the truth. Tell him, 'I grew up in foster care. I became a trafficker. But then I found Christ. I married the sheriff's daughter. I've started my own family. And now, I feel a burden for this city, and I'm doing something about it—so kids like me never go through what I did.' And after that . . . I want you to stop talking. I want you to sit there in total silence for an awkwardly long time. Not just long. Uncomfortable. Make him feel it. When he finally speaks—when his voice cracks just a little because he's trying not to cry—and he says, 'What can I do to help?' you give him one response, and only one. 'Sir, that's between you and the Lord. Take the weekend with your wife. Pray about it. And get back to me on Monday.'"

So Ron did exactly that (I've got to give him credit; he takes instruction well.) Ron delivered his pitch on a Friday. And he nailed it—he's a natural preacher, and I'm sure he stuck the landing. Then he iced the guy all weekend. Didn't follow up. Didn't poke. But Monday? Ron texted me every thirty minutes starting at 8:00 AM.

"Hasn't called yet."

"Still nothing."

"Nothing yet."

"Still waiting."

"Be calm," I finally said. "He runs an HVAC business. You know what he's doing on a Monday morning? Reviewing weekly orders. Dispatching trucks. Talking to his warehouse manager. Relax. He's not ghosting you. He's running a business."

Then, at exactly 11:00 AM, the call came.

The business owner said, "My wife and I took the weekend to pray about it, and we'd like to support you—with $50,000."

So just like that, Ron's first two capital donations were:

- $15,000 from me
- $50,000 from someone he inspired with nothing but his story and his calling

After that, Ron never looked back. He once walked into Costco, and the store manager flagged him down and handed him a check—for $700—with Costco's name on it.

"You're the only person I know who didn't give Costco $700—you got $700 from them." I told him. "Every time I go there, that's what I spend."

He does this all day, every day. Big checks. Constant support. The ministry is now well-funded and sustainable. All it took was preparation; specifically, repositioning his approach.

Now, I've worked with a lot of nonprofit founders. We've helped many increase sustainability, raise capital, and grow, but I've only seen one other story like Ron's, and that one was much more painful. That story belongs to Dr. Tammie McCafferty, who's going to be featured later in this book. For now, consider this her preview.

Tammie ran into the classic nonprofit trap: they offer too much service and never have enough money. Payroll was a challenge. Which month? Every month. So I joined her board;

I knew we needed governance-level changes. And we made three major moves.

First, we raised tuition for her flagship program, Lifework Leadership, by 50 percent. She fought me on it. She said, "No one's going to pay that." Tuition accounts for a third of her total budget. But guess what happened?

For the first time ever, she sold out the class before it started. She even had a waitlist for the following year. Why? Because the perceived value of the program went up. When people pay more, they take it more seriously.

Second, she launched a coffee ministry. This was her own idea; it now generates over $100,000 a year.

She staffs it with a mix of volunteers and formerly homeless employees. She pairs one volunteer with one person from the streets, which cuts labor costs and maximizes ministry impact. That allows most of the revenue to go directly back into Lifework Leadership. She's not Starbucks, but her model is more effective.

Third, she had to learn what Ron learned: how to raise capital. That meant sitting across from donors and asking for money—but only after showing them transformation. Just like Ron, she had to say: Here's the life change. Here's the fruit. Here's why this is worth investing in.

"I'm giving you a cause. I'm giving you results. Now I need your partnership."

That's what I told Tammie. Because like every nonprofit leader eventually faces, she had hit the same wall: her existing sponsors were fading. She went from twelve to ten to eight, and it was obvious the trajectory was downward.

So we set her up with the biggest pitch of her life—to my church. That pitch was to thirteen executives from the church, all seated around the table. All of them came from industry. Every single one had been either a vice president at a major corporation or a successful business owner.

This was a high-stakes room.

I asked Tammie, "What are you going to ask for?"

"I'm asking them for $2 million."

I blinked. "Wait. This is your first meeting with them—and you're asking for two million dollars?"

"Yeah," she said. "They have it. And I want to buy land."

"They're going to give you $2 million to buy land?"

"I need a building," she said. "With $2 million, I can buy the land and start the building."

"That's a hard no. 'Get out of my office. I don't even know why you're here,'" I said. "Look, Tammie, you're asking a church—who has a line out the door of people requesting support, including global missions—to give you $2 million to . . . buy land? How many people are coming to Jesus on the land? Is this revival land? Are we baptizing on the land? What are you doing with it? We're not doing that. Let's pick another number."

We talked it through, and she settled on $250,000, about half her annual budget. More reasonable. But even that has to come with something.

"What are you currently charging corporate sponsors?"

She said, "$10,000."

"Great. Their sponsorship is $20,000."

"But that's not a lot."

"It *is* a lot. Because when other businesses see them backing your program at $20,000, it sets a new standard. It raises your floor. It makes your sponsorship model sustainable again."

"What's the most valuable thing this church can give you?"

"People going through my program?"

"No. The most valuable thing they can give you . . . is talking about you from the stage."

This church is possibly the largest in the Southeast, maybe the country. If they mention your nonprofit from the pulpit, that's worth more than any dollar amount. That's marketing power, credibility, and kingdom reach all rolled into one.

So we made that part of the deal. $20,000, and they had to talk about her from stage.

She prepped for six months. She was mad. She cried. But she did the work. She was flexing a new muscle.

We came in with high-end, custom-printed collateral—real graphic, real visual, real professional. This is the same kind of collateral I once used to win a $25 million grant from US President Donald J. Trump. Same playbook. No PowerPoint. Just quality design and printed engineering-style documentation. She spent over $1,000, just on the printed materials for the thirteen executives.

Then she delivered her seven-minute pitch; she told her story. How she built a successful business. How she heard God's calling and sold the business. How she moved to Jacksonville. How she went to seminary and, upon graduating, took over Lifework Leadership. Lifework has now trained members of Congress and about a third of Jacksonville's elected officials. These are alumni of her program. And one thing is certain: when someone is accountable to God, you can appeal to them on that basis.

So she finished the pitch. And like any big organization would, they said, "Let us think about it."

Then they iced her for a month.

Eventually, they came back and said, "Yes. We'll do it.

But we want something."

"What's that?"

"We want to use your coffee shops to film church content anytime we want."

So that's what they got. They've now filmed four "bumper" videos in her coffee shops—including videos featuring Tim Tebow and Brock Purdy, who are both members of the church.

"That's what you get. Your coffee shops are now famous. Every week, 50,000 people across the city see them on screen. And they ask, 'Where is that?' The answer: Tammie's coffee shop, Cup of Job."

So they go. For coffee. For conversation. For Jesus. That's how you build a Kingdom business.

Ron was a quick study. It took him one week to get it, and he never looked back. Tammie's story took two years. Same lesson, same playbook. But she had to wrestle with it. It drained her. It stretched her. And she's still not fully comfortable—but she does it. She knows what she has to do now. She knows the moves. And she closed the biggest deal of her life: The Church of Eleven22. Nothing she faces is bigger than that.

Every pitch since has been smaller. Easier. Because once you've climbed Everest, every other hill is just that—a hill. She almost never calls me before meetings anymore. She's been through it. She's earned her experience base.

And now, she's not just good at doing—Tammie leads Lifework Leadership. She's also been financially successful because she didn't rely on just one approach. She stacked three strategies:

- Increased tuition (raising perceived value)
- Launched a self-sustaining coffee ministry
- Learned how to make capital asks the right way

Here's the deeper pattern behind both Ron and Tammie: There's a point in every journey where talent-stacking meets a chasm. That's the valley that stops most people. It's the gap between what you've always done and the uncomfortable, unfamiliar skill that unlocks your next level. For Ron, it was asking for capital and learning to come across with the utmost professionalism. For Tammie, it was rethinking value, presentation, and boldness.

Nobody crosses that chasm alone. That's where I came in. Not because I'm special—but because I've sold to business owners for twenty years. I've built plays that work. For Ron, it was "Matthew knows how to pivot a message." For Tammie, it was "Matthew knows how to help me diversify and stabilize my revenue."

And this brings us to Roland Udenze. Roland is a brilliant, award-winning architect. Nigerian-Irish-American, triple passport holder. And his story is a masterclass in preparation.

He started at the same company where I launched my career—Haskell. From there, in full "never say no" mode, he was recruited by PM Group out of Ireland to stand up their architectural design practice. He packed up his wife and two young kids, moved to Cork, and built their architectural arm from scratch. He designed their global headquarters: a building shaped like two hands cradling a library—a literal monument to PM Group's intellectual capital.

PM Group is no joke. They're elite. Mavericks. They dominate in China, a nearly impossible market for Western firms. Their success there tells you everything about their capability.

After Roland got the architecture practice up and running, he came back to Jacksonville. Haskell welcomed him home—but this time with a two-level promotion and full autonomy to

43

start a design studio within the company. If you're an architect, that's the dream. It's the sculptor's workshop. The painter's private studio. The place where your aesthetic becomes the product.

Roland flourished. He handpicked the most inspiring projects from Haskell's global pipeline. He won design awards—culminating with the International Project of the Year for PepsiCo's global HQ in Singapore, a three-story, ultra-sustainable manufacturing plant unlike anything else on earth.

He also brought proton therapy to the people. Roland took cold, clinical radiation tech—and made it human. He partnered with a German firm that made the magnets. Roland made the experience beautiful. He reimagined the entire feel of outpatient cancer care. Patients didn't enter a drab hospital wing. They walked into warmth. Hope. Dignity. The first three major proton therapy centers in the U.S.—that was him.

But after all that, Roland hit the ceiling. No more sponsorship. No more growth. And that's when he launched Renz Collaborative. In his fifties! But within three years, his firm was selected to design the new Atrium Health Hospital in Charlotte—the largest new hospital project in North Carolina at the time. He's never looked back.

Today, he works for me part-time; I keep him on retainer. He still gives me the "before you were famous" pricing. His exposure to automation, robotics, and manufacturing through our work gives him an edge in the healthcare world—because he brings tech fluency that most hospital designers lack. In his last project, he sold a ton of robotics. He walks into a hospital meeting and talks about what future technology can look like. People listen.

And why did he start his firm? Because he was asked to betray a client, of all things,

His boss told him, in effect, "Screw the customer or lose your job."

He chose ethics. That planted the seed. That seed grew into Renz Collaborative.

Now, when I'm pitching to architecture-forward clients, I bring Roland into the room. He pulls out high-end trace paper—parchment-like stuff. He draws with a Sharpie. Old school. Fast. He'll sketch three or four different versions in a single meeting. And each time he asks, "What do you want changed?" Layer by layer, trace paper stacked on trace paper, he keeps adjusting. And then the customer goes, "That's it. That's what I want."

I say, "Roland, tear it off. Date it. Sign it." He does. With that big, iconic, Trump-style signature of his. I roll it up, put it in a tube, hand it to the client, and say, "Hang onto this."

When the building is finally done—after code reviews, permitting, budget adjustments, robotic integrations, and endless meetings—it always looks like Roland's original sketch. Always.

Every single one of those clients frames that sketch and hangs it in their office. That's the moment the project began, when the idea became real.

Roland is charismatic. Booming voice. Contagious laugh. Better than James Earl Jones. When he speaks, I half expect the clouds to part. He's a captivating keynote speaker and brilliant creative mind, but he kept all of that bottled up for almost three decades—until he realized the only way to maximize his impact was to go out on his own.

And that's the point. Whether it's Ron, or Tammie, or Roland—or maybe you—there's a season of preparation, followed by a defining decision. When that moment comes, the only question that matters is this: *Are you ready to act?*

MATTHEW CHANG

# CHAPTER 3

# STUDY, PRAY, SERVE

**Y**OU'VE DONE THE PREPARATION. YOU'VE BEEN a great employee. And now the question becomes: *Are you spiritually fortified?* Before you take on risk—before you step into leadership—you need to be rooted. Because risk-taking will absolutely bring leadership challenges. And it will expose ethical dilemmas. If you're not grounded in something stronger than your own ambition, you will get pulled off course.

How do you become spiritually fortified? It's simple: Study. Pray. Serve.

Read the Bible—not just once. Keep reading it. Sit with it. Ask God, *Open the doors You want open. Close the doors You want closed.* And finally, you serve. Put yourself in a position where you're the hands and feet of someone else's vision, not your own. His vision.

Through that process—through studying, praying, and serving—you'll build inner resilience that no thunder can quiver. You will be tough. You will be firm. And you will be decisive. You'll need that clarity. Because when the pressure comes, the world will give you all kinds of advice. So will your attorney. So will your emotions.

In 2022, I faced my first ever lawsuits—four federal lawsuits headed to trial. I'd never been in a lawsuit before. Now it was all happening at once. So what do you do? Well, you don't panic. You don't act out of fear. And you sure don't ever, *ever* compromise.

You exemplify Christ. That was the only prayer I had through that whole ordeal: *God, let me act like Jesus. Let my conduct glorify You.* And we won. All four cases—including full recovery of principal plus attorneys' fees. And just as importantly, we never did anything that would be an embarrassment or trigger a PR crisis. We were spiritually fortified before the storm hit. That's the key. Now, let me give it to you.

## STUDY, PRAY, SERVE

When I teach these at my church or to employees (yes, that's what we do at Chang Robotics), I cover them in reverse order. Let's begin.

### Serve

This is the number one thing I see missing in people who have big aspirations. They've read the books. They've listened to the podcasts. They've mapped out the future. But they haven't served. And that's the easiest step of all. Most assumed steps are unnecessary or redundant. You don't need a résumé to serve. You don't need a certification to serve. You'll be trained as you serve. You just need you, who like so many saints and heroes of the Bible said, "Here I am, send me."

Look, every nonprofit you admire is desperate for volunteers. Service is simple; there are only two requirements:

**One, have fun.** Walk in the door with energy, a good attitude, and a willingness to help. At my church, we call our volunteers "serve staff." *What's your job?* OK, then, we just need you to . . .

**Two, do what you're told, and do it joyfully.** Ego-check at the door. Let someone else lead.

This is the critical mental shift. Service is not about being a visionary. It's not your mission, your plan, or your timeline. You're following someone else's lead for the good of others.

Now, I always recommend that people start small with service. Not with, say, a high-status yet psychologically exhausting board position, but with actual, physical, recurring service. Real, hard work. Something that happens on a schedule. Something where other people are counting on you to show up.

At Chang Robotics, we believe in tithing our time. Every team member is encouraged to serve outside of work. But it only means something if you follow through and keep doing so. Many service roles require a multi-year commitment. If you sign up to lead a middle school youth group, don't just show up for one semester. You pick up those kids in sixth grade, build relationships, earn trust . . . and walk them all the way through eighth grade. That's a three-year commitment. High school is four years. It's a lot, but the reward is greater. Relationships form through recurring contact. That's what Jared Bynum taught me.

So if you're looking for your next step . . .

If you feel like you're waiting on God to show you the path . . .

He already told you where to begin:

**Serve.**

## Pray

The second spiritual fortification is prayer. One of the best ways to develop your prayer life is, unironically, through serving others. When you're in close proximity to other people's real lives, you begin to understand the weight they're carrying. You stop assuming. You start listening.

If you make a habit of asking, "How can I pray for you?"—you gain a lens into how other people think. You begin to understand what burdens them. What they're afraid of. What they hope for. and often, what feels trivial to you might be monumental to them. That's the foundation of empathy, and empathy is not optional for leaders.

One of my favorite groups to pray with is teachers and nurses. To the outside world, their requests might seem small—a change in school policy, or a new hospital procedure. But when you listen with empathy, you realize how those "small" changes can shake the foundation of their daily life. You begin to see how institutional decisions feel personal to the people on the frontlines. That changes how you lead.

Prayer is more than feeling; it's faith. If your prayers are small, it might be because your picture of God is small. Big prayers reflect belief in a big God. Here's how I structure mine:

- **Personal prayers**. I pray by name for every family member's health. And I also pray for each person in my extended family who, to my knowledge, does not yet know Jesus—that God would woo them unto Himself.
- **City-sized prayers**. I pray for my pastor, my mayor, and every elected official in my city. That they would be washed in the blood of Christ and make decisions led by the Spirit.

- **Nation-sized prayers.** I've prayed for every president since Barack Obama. I pray that our national leaders—regardless of who's in power—would lead under the covering of the blood of Christ. Their burdens are heavier than we can imagine. They need spiritual strength. They need wisdom. And they need our prayers more than they need our opinions.

This has become a daily rhythm for me. I believe prayer is a skill—something you grow into, something you practice. The Bible gives us both models and mentors in prayer. For example, King David prayed with raw humility and fierce confidence. His Psalms reflect a heart that fully depended on God—whether in defeat or victory. David never won a battle he should have won. Every win was God showing up.

Jesus Christ taught us exactly how to pray under the New Covenant with, "Our Father. . ." Prayer is relational and direct and powerful. We're to pray for daily provision, forgiveness, protection, and above all—for God's will to be done.

If you've never developed a consistent prayer life, start now. Pray small. Pray big. Pray with humility. Pray with boldness. But above all—pray like you believe God is listening. He is.

## Study

Now, in terms of study, there is a lot of potential material for you, both in the Bible text and by commentators who have unpacked the Bible for specific themes. I believe the Bible is powerful when it comes to conflict and battle. One resource I've found especially encouraging is the framing of the Psalms by the music artists Shane & Shane—specifically their *Psalms Live* album. Especially for men, it's a powerful tool that teaches how to engage with scripture. Their songs are based directly on the biblical Psalms, and they become both a cry for shelter under God, and a rejoicing in God's power—while being humbled by His almighty sovereignty. These are important concepts for study, especially when facing conflict.

Another teaching that's had a major impact on me is the idea of doing money God's way. Consider downloading your bank statements and categorizing every expense from the previous three months. *Where your money goes, your heart follows.* When you actually study your own spending, it reveals your true priorities. Most people are surprised—*How much went to Amazon? How much to the bar? To golf?* And how little to generosity, self-improvement, or investing in assets?

So, my main point is this: **You just have to study** (where your time goes, your heart follows.) Now, the best way to start is with daily Bible reading. Easier said than done, yeah. Daily Bible reading is difficult—if not impossible—for most Christians without help. For me, it's simple: my church sends me a daily excerpt that's aligned with our weekly teaching. I just follow along. Another great resource is the classic devotional *My Utmost for His Highest*, which I did back in my early twenties. It helped me uncover deeper meaning in Scripture beyond just the surface level.

And of course, there's the "Read-the-Bible-in-a-Year" programs. These are excellent because they give you a complete overview. You can say you've read it cover to cover, and you begin to understand how the entire story flows. Most of these programs include both Old Testament and New Testament readings each day. And in my view, the Old Testament's primary role is to point forward to the New—so reading both together is essential for context.

Now, I'll admit: I'm not someone who memorizes Scripture in large chunks. I know people who have hundreds of verses committed to memory, and that gives them powerful resources in conflict or debate. For me, it's more meaningful to understand the meta-concepts of the Bible—how it fits together, what the historical context is, and what the bigger picture looks like.

That's why, in our family, we've expanded our study through travel. We've taken several trips to better understand the story of the Bible and the context in which it was written. The most impactful was a trip to the Middle East. We spent three weeks starting in Egypt, visiting all the major historical sites—pyramids, Pharaoh carvings, and more. Egypt plays a central role in the Bible, and I wanted to understand: *What were the Hebrews doing there?*

Interestingly, modern Egyptian history does not mention the Hebrews. I asked several Egyptologists. They said, "Yes, we agree the Hebrews lived here. They were honored guests, and we treated them well."

So I asked, "Did they build anything for you?" I was standing at the foot of the Grand Pyramid when I asked this.

They replied, "Oh no, there's no record of that. But it's likely they helped with building—and we certainly paid them well."

Amusing.

Egypt is also home to one of the oldest branches of Christianity: the Coptic Church. While Coptic Christians are only about 10 percent of the population, they hold most of the financial and political power in Egypt.

From Egypt, we traveled to Israel, where we took a Messianic Jew-guided tour led by Jewish believers in Jesus. We visited all the major biblical locations, including the

Golan Heights. In 2017, while standing at the Syrian border, I witnessed ISIS convoys on the other side. I saw the infamous white Toyota trucks from all the videos. My instinct was to hide behind our tour bus—my wife was pregnant with our first child. But the tour guide said, "Relax. They won't do anything. They want to keep existing." That experience gave me . . . perspective.

We also visited Capernaum—center of most Gospel activity—as well as Nazareth and Cana. We swam in the Sea of Galilee. While out on the water, during a teaching about Jesus calming the storm, a wind actually picked up over what had been a calm sea. It was surreal.

We then stayed in Palestine, in the West Bank. We did homestays with Palestinian Christians, visited local schools, and shared meals with families. That gave me a completely different understanding of modern conflict. The people we met—Muslims and Christians alike—were warm, generous, and deeply rooted in their culture. It reminded me not to trust the headlines.

We even visited the Bethlehem Brewery—yes, there's a functioning brewery in Palestine. And in Jerusalem, we stayed near the Mount of Olives, which also happens to have the best falafel in Israel. We toured underground Jerusalem and saw archeological remains connected to the Gospel stories, like the pool where Jesus healed the paralyzed man.

We also traveled to East Africa, one of the most aid-saturated yet still-impoverished regions on earth. Uganda alone has over 55,000 NGOs. We stayed in orphanages where all the children had been rescued from witchcraft, some of them having experienced demonic possession. I personally witnessed a supernatural event in a church that had blended Christianity and witchcraft—deeply unsettling and deeply real.

We visited rehabilitation clinics for sex trafficking victims, many of whom were orphaned during the Rwandan genocide. These women had lived two decades in the sex trade. Now they were being set free—finding healing, finding Jesus, and finding community.

We also went to Malaysia, specifically Malacca, a Christian city in a Muslim-majority country. It has a fascinating colonial history: Portuguese, Dutch, and British. Malacca was once the most important port in the region before Singapore was founded. There are still Portuguese Catholics living there today.

Seeing Christianity's influence across the globe—through travel, people, architecture—has radically deepened my understanding of Scripture. It's one thing to read the Bible. It's another thing entirely to walk where the stories happened, meet the people affected, and understand the real-world ripple effects of the Great Commission.

That's what study looks like to me. Not just reading. But understanding. Seeking. Living it.

As for you, consider the following path: Sign up for a short-term international mission trip. I'm serious; do it. A short-term mission trip—especially when experienced through the eyes of the local people and long-term missionaries on the ground—is, in my opinion, the single best way to deepen your understanding of the Bible. It aligns directly with the Great Commission.

But the real purpose of a short-term mission trip isn't to change the people in the country you're visiting. It's to change you. It's your heart that gets reshaped. One week of pseudo-service and temporary help won't radically alter their situation—but it can radically change your perspective.

There's a "skill stack" that comes with going on a trip

like this. First, you have to tell people you're going. You'll be explaining to friends, coworkers, and family why you're going and what you hope to accomplish. That in itself is a powerful act of evangelism—publicly declaring what you believe, and more importantly, showing you're taking action based on that belief.

Second, short-term mission trips are often expensive—usually between $3,000 and $7,000. You'll need to raise support. That means asking others to help fund your mission. That's a form of capital raising, which we've already talked about earlier in this book. For many people, it's the first time they've had to ask for money for something they believe in. And it's an experience that's humbling—and revealing.

For me personally, I was completely surprised by who stepped up and supported my first trip... and who didn't. The people I expected to back me up disappeared. Meanwhile, people I never would've guessed quietly gave—generously. I still remember one soft-spoken colleague from Haskell who, after hearing about my first trip to Africa, handed me a $500 check. I was floored.

As I publicized my trip to my workplace, I shared updates with my team. The CEO of Haskell took notice and told me something that stuck with me, "If you come up short, come see me last. I'll cover the rest."

This was a $4,500 trip in 2014—expensive because it was going to Africa. I raised $3,000 but came up $1,500 short.

So I went into his office and said, "Do you remember the promise you made?"

He smiled and said, "Yes."

On the spot, he wrote the final check. He didn't subscribe to my version of faith, but he admired the courage it took to go where I was going and to do what I said I believed in.

Those moments taught me lessons I'll never forget: how to speak boldly about your beliefs, how to raise funds for a mission-driven cause, and, maybe most importantly, how to be humbled by the people who show up to support you when you least expect it. And *that* is all worth studying.

## BUT WHY?

Why *Serve, Pray, Study*, specifically? Because when you serve, you get over yourself. When you pray, you get beyond yourself. And when you study, you stop trusting only yourself. Together, these disciplines form a spiritual infrastructure. They humble you. They lift your gaze. They make you brave. They make you useful. And when hardship, lawsuits, betrayals, business failures, or ethical dilemmas hit—as they inevitably will—you have a foundation to stand on that isn't made of sand.

Now, *how* do these three personal spiritual practices fortify you, you might wonder? They make you comfortable with the uncomfortable, which is necessary for success in entrepreneurship, or really in any endeavor.

Story time now. Dr. Nahshon Nicks, whom I teased earlier in the book, is both a servant and a student. He's a well-built, self-disciplined man—a black belt in mixed martial arts and a successful amateur MMA fighter. And he has not one, but two doctorates in divinity. He's the kind of leader who's willing to work hard under the right mentorship. But that willingness was tested when a personal mentor betrayed him. That betrayal drove him inward, toward self-reliance. And from that place, he launched one of the most exciting grassroots campaigns in Jacksonville's recent political history.

Dr. Nicks ran for city council. He's a respected black community leader—and that's when the Democratic Party turned on him. The Democratic National Committee's local attorney sued to kick him off the ballot, telling him directly and in no uncertain terms, *We have enough of you. This time we want a gay.*

Fortunately, that wasn't the end of the story. He found his way forward—mentorship, this time with me—and we brought in backup: Ron DeSantis's election integrity attorney, a man known around here as "The Gunslinger," a Jewish Matlock with a reputation for strategic firepower. They dropped the case; Dr. Nicks stayed on the ballot. He won 28,000 votes in the primary. His campaign cost far less than $10,000—just $0.07 cents per vote.

He didn't win the seat, but Nahshon had his day at the ballot box, which was the springboard for everything that came next. His own party tried to erase him. He refused to go quietly. He was later appointed to the mayor's transition council and is now one of the most effective forces in local politics, for good. Nahshon then went on to found Team Nitro, a local non-profit that teaches K-12 children the discipline and self confidence that comes from martial arts. He teaches the students self-defense and about the love of Jesus. The city has funded Nahshon's non-profit with more than $1 million over a multi-year contract.

Nothing prepares you for being sued by your own party. No ordinary citizen is ready for hit pieces in the press, attack ads, public lies, or having your wife falsely accused of abusing a VA loan—especially when she's a disabled veteran. But Nahshon never folded.

He worked with what he had. And he made it count. 28,000

votes. Less than $10,000. And a public reputation that no political machine could erase. Now, Nahshon is unstoppable. Few are fortified like this man.

Spiritual fortification is like strength training, as a matter of fact. And if we break it down further—because obviously I love working out—there's both the discomfort of the workout itself and the lingering discomfort that follows. When you're working out, you're pushing through heart rate, effort, physical strain—for, say, an hour. Then there's the soreness that can last five, six, sometimes seven days after a hard workout.

I think both types of discomfort apply to spiritual preparation. There's the momentary discomfort—like that initial awkwardness of serving in a ministry for the first time. For example, "I don't know how to relate to students," or "What if I seem too old, or not cool enough?" You feel unqualified. Unready.

And then there's lingering discomfort, which is that ongoing tension as you try to get comfortable in the role and gain confidence. I've seen this again and again: highly qualified professionals—top of their class, killing it at work—who suddenly feel totally unqualified to serve food in a homeless shelter.

Or they say, "I've never struggled with addiction, so how could I possibly serve in addiction recovery?"

That's normal. That's human. But what those communities need most isn't perfection; it's authenticity. Show up. Make eye contact. Listen. Take people seriously. That's what builds relationships. And over time—sometimes a year or more—that lingering discomfort fades as you find your footing.

It's the same with prayer. Developing your prayer life takes repetition and boldness. Learning to pray in a way that reflects the size of the God you believe in. A small God leads to small prayers. Ask for big things from your big God.

And study? That discomfort hits when the Bible confronts you with truths you didn't expect. It challenges your assumptions. It shows you how to love, how to forgive, how to submit, how to fight. And, just like in the gym, you need that daily discipline. You start small, stay consistent, and gain strength over time.

All of this prepares you to pick up something heavy later. That's the point. Serving, prayer, and study build spiritual and emotional muscle. You'll have the foundation—and the reps—so that when it's time to lead or launch or risk, you're ready.

Now, like in weightlifting, there's a safety factor, too. Just because you can pick something up doesn't mean it's wise. Maybe you can lift that weight once, but you'll hurt yourself and be out for a month. The goal is sustainable growth. You learn your limits, and you grow wisely. Some people take on too much. They say yes to everything and end up overwhelmed. I don't struggle with this personally—I just keep going—but many of my key staff over the years have. For them, we've had to manage workload carefully. Otherwise, they risk burnout or even a PTSD-like response due to the pressure. This stage of preparation is critical because it reveals what you can handle—and when to ask for help or slow down.

It's all part of the training. So when you eventually get the call to pick up something big, you'll already be strong enough. And you'll know what *heavy* feels like when you do.

# CHAPTER 4

# START SMALL, PLAY BIG

**S**TARTING SMALL ALLOWS YOU TO ACQUIRE critical skills before the big moment arrives. You play like you practice. During your season of study and prayer, you may begin to sense an "itch"—a spiritual nudge, a call, a restlessness. That's often the Holy Spirit prompting you that something is coming. Use this time to practice leadership before it really matters.

## PRACTICAL WAYS TO START SMALL

- **Serve...more**. Put yourself in a position to be the hands and feet of a higher authority outside your workplace. Start with something unpaid. If you consistently serve for a year or two, you will almost *always* be offered a leadership role. Service fortifies you spiritually; it's always a sure path to more responsibility. Sometimes, *lots* of responsibility. It's OK to start small, but it's probably not OK to stay that way.

- **Start a business**. At Chang Robotics, we expect all employees to have at minimum a side business. I'll spend most of the rest of this chapter on this one bullet alone because there is so much that needs to be said about starting an eventually successful enterprise, small.

- **Join a board**. For me, it started with our HOA. It wasn't until I became an entrepreneur that I began joining nonprofit boards, but you don't have to wait. Everyone has access to small governance opportunities—PTA, HOA, ministry teams, or community task forces.

I joined our HOA because we had a 19-building condo complex, mostly retirees, and a major renovation on the horizon. The new assessment would have dramatically increased living costs, pricing out many residents. It was a politically sensitive situation—so many Karens to manage. It taught me diplomacy fast.

When you do a good job but still get criticized, you start learning what leadership really means. Most employees never experience that. They say things like, "But I worked hard!" or "It's not fair!"—things you'll never hear from a real leader. Leaders don't whine. They shoulder the burden, take the blame, and keep moving. Nothing quite teaches that like working the HOA, with one exception. And that exception is entrepreneurship.

# STARTING A SMALL BUSINESS, NOT PLAYING SMALL

When I started Chang Robotics, I had already started four businesses—most of which had generated revenue but eventually failed. This is because I was doing them on the side, while keeping a "real job." So I personally didn't think, for many years, that starting a side hustle works for most people—at least not as the path to a serious business.

Now, a lot has changed since I formed that opinion. The gig economy didn't exist back then, but today, it does offer people a legitimate path to test their skills and build something real. So I think the options today look more like this:

## Three Entrepreneurship Options

Option **one** is to enter the gig economy. Hang out your shingle for whatever you think your expertise is. Go through the full cycle:

1. Find your first (potential) customer.
2. Explain what you do.
3. Handle objections.
4. Ask for the sale (and close)
5. Follow through on delivery.
6. Ask for referrals.

Starting your own company is not a strict requirement at Chang Robotics, but I ask every team member to have at least one secondary income stream or side hustle. I want them to think like owners. I want them to feel what it's like to be responsible for outcomes—not just collect a paycheck. Results have been fascinating. My marketing team, a group of young women in their early twenties, started their own marketing agency. I encouraged them, sent them free guides I'd found online, and gave them room to experiment. Sure enough, there was a two-month dip in their performance at my company—because they had early success. They found clients willing to pay them thousands for marketing services. Then, around the five or six-month mark, they came to me for advice—not about their work for me, but about how to manage the angry customers they'd accumulated. That's when they learned some real lessons. They hadn't defined their service scope. They didn't understand customer service or what it takes to make a business owner happy when they're paying you *real* money. And so, they gained a whole new level of respect for what we do at Chang Robotics—and what they get here. They started treating our clients as if they were their own. They became more grateful, more mature. They no longer took the structure around them for granted—finance, operations, execution—they could just focus on marketing. They realized what a gift their jobs are.

We've had people start side hustles as ranchers, homebuilders, farmers, taxi drivers, and private consultants. What always ends up happening is they come back with a deeper appreciation for what they have. And that's the whole point of my system. If someone discovers that they can thrive better on their own, I want that for them. But if, through experience, they discover their highest and best potential is as part of my team . . . we've crossed a major bridge together. And those become loyal team members for life.

Now, your **second** entrepreneurship option is starting a family business. All *that* really requires is a good credit score.

With it, you can buy an investment property and rent it out, or buy into a franchise.

Now, you've probably seen the talk online about "retiring your wife." Well, sure—you can "retire her" into the family business; let her run the franchise or be your property manager. What that really means is you'll have a new depth of dinner table conversation, reviewing debt documents and operations manuals and discussing the best way to dispel employee drama. You'll both grow. It's stressful, but if your marriage can handle it, you'll find every conversation empowering. For the both of you.

I've come to believe that starting a family business is one of the best toe-in-the-water ways to learn entrepreneurship. It gives you skin in the game, but you're not doing it alone—and you can learn the ropes in a hands-on way.

A **third** way you can get started as a private individual is by saving enough capital to invest in someone else's company. A small business buy-in usually starts around $25,000. If you're able to save up that amount, there's a good chance you can partner with someone whose vision you believe in. It's a great way to test your skills—not just as an investor, but as someone who bets on people.

That's what small business investing really is: You're betting on people. And if you bring some domain expertise to the table, your support becomes even more valuable. You might be great at accounting, legal, sales, or marketing—whatever it is, you can offer that to the founder, often at no cost, and help them succeed while building your own experience at the same time.

So to review, those three on-ramps to entrepreneurship are:

1. Participate in the gig economy.

2. Start a family business.
3. Invest in someone else's company.

## SMALL MINISTRY, BIG IMPACT

Now, if your ambitions are to eventually go into ministry full time, the best move for future leaders is to cross-train inside a larger organization. We've already talked in this book about how fundraising and operational logistics can be very uncomfortable for gifted ministers. The solution is to broaden your exposure—develop competence in operations, volunteer coordination, compliance, financial management, and donor relations. Expertise like that. You may not naturally gravitate toward these, but they're critical. You won't launch or lead a healthy nonprofit without them.

Another highly strategic move ministers can make is building relationships with business owners. You will have successful people in your flock, people who own companies and understand leadership in the private sector. Offer to be their workplace chaplain. Lead a Bible study, prayer group, or devotional on site. It's a powerful way to serve while gaining real exposure to how businesses operate day to day.

And there's a bonus: Those business leaders often become your mentors—and potentially your early funders—when the time comes for you to launch your own ministry. I recommend aspiring ministry leaders establish at least **four** such relationships. That's just one business visit per week. In a given month, you'll rotate through all four. It's not a distraction from your core ministry; it's an apprenticeship in the real world. And the lessons you'll learn there will serve you when it's time to step out on your own.

And whether you're in business or ministry, you'll need to **network**. Now, we'll cover this in full in Chapter 6. But starting small, starting right now, there is a particular kind of networking you'll do.

# HOW TO START NETWORKING RIGHT

The easiest way to start small is to join a **trade association** or an **affinity group**.

A trade association connects directly to your profession. For me, that's the American Society of Civil Engineers. In a group like that, you'll meet both independent business owners and journeyman professionals—people at various stages in the career arc. Some might become mentors. Others could become employees, partners, or advisors later in your journey. These associations usually meet once a month, so it's a low-commitment, high-exposure way to start building relationships.

Now, an affinity group could be something like a technology club or Toastmasters. These aren't tied to your industry, but they'll connect you with people who are good at something you want to get better at. In Jacksonville, we have an affinity group called Jax Tech. Who shows up there? Anybody interested in tech. What counts as tech? That's up to you—software, robotics, GIS, AI—it all fits. What matters is the people you meet; you'll find others on the same journey, and others further ahead who can show you the road.

Now, if you're in Toastmasters, for example, you'll meet seasoned speakers—and beginners just trying to speak with confidence. It's an ideal environment for skill-building. And you might realize you're further along than you thought—or that you've got a ways to go. Maybe you're still terrified of being called on in a meeting, or maybe you're not even sure how to describe what you do. That's good to know now. It's like the gym; no one walks in on day one and deadlifts 400 pounds. You figure out where you are, set the target, and build a plan you can stick to.

And my favorite benefit of this entry-level networking is **the immediate prevention of wasted efforts**. You'll learn pretty quick how to avoid unnecessary mistakes, wasted time, and discouragement. You can borrow what works, skip what doesn't, and move faster. Plenty of people will be glad to tell you everything that they know . . . that doesn't work. So you can avoid it. From the beginning of your journey is this endeavor.

Now, this idea of "wasted effort" merits a little more attention. Because sometimes, this worry is industrial-grade "cope." As in, an attempt to cope with and otherwise explain away an excuse. You see, some people are so afraid of wasting time—especially if they already have a full-time job, a family, or other responsibilities—that they start *too* small. But starting too big can be overwhelming, too.

There is a healthy balance. The title of the book shows us: *Risk-Taking Is Biblical*. You're probably starting at the right size when the risk feels heavy on your heart. Not necessarily heavy on your calendar but heavy on your heart. You feel the weight of it. That said, before you take that leap, it's vital to do your self-assessment and find people like you who've done what you're about to do. That's how you calibrate your starting point.

Here's a personal example. I learned how to swim as an adult. Not "I didn't know how to stay afloat"—but lap swimming, for time, proper form. My wife is an elite swimmer, so asking her for advice felt like asking Michael Phelps how to shave five seconds off your lap. He might say, "Kick harder, breathe less." Thanks. Not helpful.

What I needed was someone like me: another adult who'd started from zero and worked their way up. In my case, it was a 6'6", 300-pound former D1 athlete who gave me one tip—to change the way I held my hands in the water. That single tip dropped ten seconds off my lap time. Because he had to learn it the hard way, just like I was doing.

The point of start-small networking is to help with figuring out where you are and who you can learn from. As another example, you're not going to get useful startup advice from Elon Musk. He's not you. You need someone who was where you are, just a few years ago, with a similar background and similar resources. Same with weightlifting. You're not going to train with Ronnie Coleman. Even if you could, it wouldn't help. What you want is someone a bit further down the path who started where you did—and can tell you what works at your level.

## START SMALL, NETWORK BIG, GROW BIGGER

Someone I'd like to highlight (again) here is Dr. Tammie McClafferty. She's done an excellent job of curating a mix of people in her life—some who are diligent, and others who are extraordinary. She surrounds herself with successful, hardworking people whose diligence she can easily replicate. She's naturally a hard worker, so when someone gives her the playbook or the business plan, she can run with it.

But she also keeps a smaller circle of people who challenge her—who expose where she needs to grow. I've already mentioned how she struggled with and didn't love: fundraising. But she's now at the point where she can stick the pitch and close major donors. That growth didn't happen by accident. It happened because she curated the right mix of people—those who inspire her faithfulness and consistency, and those who push her to expand her skills.

Right now, for instance, she's doubling the size of her board of directors and dramatically increasing its quality. Each new board member is bringing something she wasn't already good at. One example is digital marketing. Tammie didn't grow up in the internet era, so things like social media and SEO felt like a wall to her—confusing and overwhelming. Her first reaction used to be, "I'm not good at social media." Or, "I don't do websites." But now, she surrounds herself with people who are excellent digital storytellers and media strategists. She's brought on board members who are Christ-loving leaders with expertise in SEO and content strategy. She recognized, in as many words, I'm not going to be the person who builds this. But I can surround myself with the people who do. A little networking goes a long way.

Tammie's career really took off when she and her husband opened a daycare in Pennsylvania. It was a competitive market, and they made it work. Eventually, they expanded to five daycare centers. Both of them left their day jobs to run the business full-time.

Now, Tammie and her husband are both ministry-minded. They weren't great at compliance and state reporting—essential elements of running a daycare in any state—but they were great at running the facilities and keeping families happy.

That's what brought them success.

Then, through prayer and study of the Scriptures, they felt a calling from God to leave private business and pursue full-time ministry. So they sold the daycare business, moved to Jacksonville, Florida, and enrolled together in seminary. They had no plan beyond that, beyond obedience to what they felt as God's call. And so, they both earned master's degrees in theology. After seminary, Tammie was offered the executive director role at Lifework Leadership; her husband became an executive pastor at a local church.

Since then, Tammie has earned her doctorate in theology and become that "Dr. McCafferty" I introduced you to. She's been leading Lifework for eight years, as of this writing. In that time, she's tripled the organization's revenue, increased enrollment by around 20 percent, and cultivated an alumni network that includes US congressmen, city councilors, and CEOs. Those relationships now expand the influence of Lifework far beyond what it was when she started there.

Tammie's journey is a textbook example of starting small—open one daycare—then scaling by obedience and discipline. She stepped away at the height of success to pursue ministry. And now, God is blessing her a second time in a second act.

I humbly submit that I started small with Chang Robotics as well. For the first four years, we didn't focus on sales or marketing at all. Our website was literally . . . a blog. If you visited it, you'd only find articles I'd written. Nothing to buy. No description of who we were or what we offered. Just my uncensored thoughts on tech.

In those early years, we focused only on two things: serving clients and designing great projects. We wanted to do whatever it took to serve clients well and build award-winning, excellent engineering solutions.

One outcome of that service mindset is a great example of starting small and scaling impact. During the COVID-19 pandemic, Chang Robotics published the national industrial hygiene standard that allowed factories and job sites to stay open. That standard started as a plan for one single job site: our biggest one. We were told by the governor of South Carolina that all construction sites would pause. That would've meant lost revenue and layoffs.

So out of necessity, we asked, "How are hospitals still open?" We studied OSHA's bloodborne disease plans. We studied hospital ER infectious disease protocols (thanks to my ER wife!). We built our own plan, submitted it to the client, and they passed it to the lieutenant governor of South Carolina. It was approved. That plan, other construction companies used as well.

"Do you mind if we share it with all the manufacturers in South Carolina?" the client asked us.

Our motto at Chang Robotics is, "Safety has no price." So we don't sell safety. There's no IP in safety. So I said, "Of course. You're free to use it."

That same client then asked if they could expand the standard to all seventeen of their factories across North America. Yes, of course. And so, the plan spread through their entire network. Then I got a cold call from the US Trade Consulate.

"We've received your COVID safety document. Would you allow us to share it with our members?"

Their membership includes every US manufacturer—basically every Fortune 1,000 company. From there, it spread even further, internationally. Some of the content and structure of our document was eventually adopted into OSHA and CDC guidance on industrial hygiene during the pandemic.

That all came out of an act of service—one job site, one plan. We were trying to protect our people and keep the job moving.

And that was the "energy" of our first four years—keeping our heads down, delivering engineering excellence, building a great team, serving clients with pride. No sales pitch. No marketing.

After that early near-acquisition attempt I described earlier, I realized we had to be completely self-reliant—sales, finance, legal, banking, all of it. Once Chang Robotics had proof of concept—once we'd demonstrated we could serve clients, deliver exceptional work, and lead a world-class team—then we started telling the world. That's when public recognition began rolling in. In 2024, Chang Robotics was the only company selected by *Inc.* Magazine and *Fast Company* as "Best in the Business" in robotics.

We truly started small. Only after we'd proven ourselves did we begin scaling. That's the phase we're in now, as I am writing this very book.

Now, that's probably inspiring, but you probably have a question now: *How do I keep from staying small?*

Good question.

## HOW TO AVOID STAYING SMALL

When it comes to timelines, milestones, urgency, and so forth, consider the power of **cycles**. Most people don't like change. That's why *Who Moved My Cheese?* is a perennial bestseller. But annual cycles—seasons—are baked into how we live. We file taxes annually. We set goals for the new year. We celebrate birthdays and holidays once a year. And I believe risk-taking is an annual rhythm, too.

So, let's say in year one, you just focus on going to affinity groups and trade association meetings. Show up, once a month, for a year. Build a reputation. That's a start.

If you're planning to start a business, maybe your year-one goal is to save up $25,000 in seed capital. That's measurable. It's achievable in one to two years for most working Americans. And during that time, improve your credit score. Because if you ever want a bank loan to launch your dream, you'll need it. Credit score is your resume when it comes to financing.

For ministry, it might be cross-training. If you're at a large organization, then in year one or two, you should be able to rotate through several departments—finance, volunteer coordination, development, compliance—and learn how everything works.

The key is setting one-year targets, tracking them, and executing them. I learned from a business mentor to track what we call your "say/do ratio." That's the percentage of things you say you're going to do that you actually follow through on.

You want a one-to-one. That's perfect. Never make deals with anyone who runs under 50 percent, meaning for every two things they say they'll do, they only follow through on one of them, on average. These people will disappoint you. More importantly, turning the attention to you now, if you want to be a leader or entrepreneur, you've got to prove to yourself that you're capable of doing what you say.

I'll conclude with this: Three years is the outer limit for preparation. If you're already serving, already speaking, already doing something active in your community . . . you might be ready to take your risk in just one year. But if you're starting from cold, if you're brand new to this risk-taker's mindset, then three years is your max prep window. After that, it's go-time. Scale up, no matter what. Jesus built the world's greatest movement in just three years with only a rag-tag group of disciples.

Speaking of Jesus, this brings us right back to the parable of the talents. The man with five didn't sit on them, wait for perfect timing, or hoard them until he found the "right opportunity." He invested the first one, then the second. He started—then kept going until every. single. one. was invested.

You don't wait until you feel like it. You don't wait until you're 100 percent ready (which is *cope* anyway.) You don't wait until your plan is perfect. You go.

Along the way, you'll meet people who want to help you.

To meet them, turn the page.

**MATTHEW CHANG**

# CHAPTER 5

# ACCUMULATE WISE MENTORS

**PRESIDENT BARACK OBAMA INFAMOUSLY SAID OF SMALL** business owners and entrepreneurs in America, "You didn't build that." Conservative media mocked him for it, but I agree—well, almost. Because a follow-up line, added by Democrat leaders trying to help the president save face, was "You didn't build that *by yourself*." That's where I wholeheartedly agree.

No, I did not get where I am by myself. I was born into a household with married parents in the United States. That's the ideal head start right there—stability, love, structure, and opportunity. None of us choose our own personal starting line. But at the same time, the person who builds something—who risks their savings, reputation, time, and energy to create something out of nothing—is a visionary risk-taker. Ultimately, they bear the burden. When it fails, no one else feels it like they do. And when it succeeds, no one else made it happen in quite the same way.

If you want to go far, you must surround yourself with people who've gone farther. Older, wiser individuals who've faced failure, come back from it, and who can point out pitfalls before you even see them. One of the biggest mistakes I see in aspiring entrepreneurs and early-stage risk-takers is that they haven't built a support system in advance. They're waiting for the storm before they decide to get shelter.

Mentorship doesn't work that way. You have to build your bench early; you need to know a guy. Better yet, know the guy who knows the *guys*. If you play your cards right, one day you'll be that guy others turn to.

Before I launched Chang Robotics, I proactively reached out to ten experienced engineering and design firm founders and asked them to mentor me. I understood human psychology well enough to know not all would say yes—and that was fine. In the end, ten accepted. Five didn't become mentors; they offered me a job. And three offered me equity positions, inviting me to join them as a partner or co-owner. That's what happens when you lead with humility, a learner's mindset, and the boldness to ask.

Let me tell you a little more of how mentorship happened to and for me—and along the way, I'll teach you how to find mentors yourself. One day, you may just become *their* mentor. I want to linger on that point before we move on, actually. You see, ultimately, what can happen in mentorship is that you become the mentor to your mentor—or at least, you graduate to co-equal status. That's a successful mentorship. And that's happened to me several times. In some cases, I've surpassed my mentors and become theirs, but the relationship stays healthy. I still haven't caught up to any of my mentors in terms of wisdom or emotional discipline. Two of my most formative mentors—both of them former university deans—now work at my company. I still call them when I need a sounding board. They answer.

## THE TWO QUESTIONS

When you meet people who are in a position you'd like to be in—and it could just be one attribute of their life, like their marriage, technical acumen (in my case), or their ability to start a business with returning customers—do two things:

1. Bring them value. *What can I do to help that potential mentor?*

2. Ask them questions when facing an important decision. (Essentially, I'm letting them be my mentor with training wheels on by informally asking them for advice.)

At Chang Robotics, we base our understanding of mentorship on the book *The Go-Giver*. We call it "give to give", meaning to give away value simply because you are a giver. In the professional world, most often, what we have to give is value. Here's a simple example: When I was recruiting mentors, if I happened to be at a trade show and saw something interesting, I would send a quick text or email to the prospective mentor with a picture and a short summary of what I found, and I'd ask them directly, "Is this something I can work on for you?" or, "Is there an introduction I can make here?"

Notice I have their mentorship of me in mind, but I lead with value. I give to give. First, I found something potentially useful or interesting. Second, I was in a place they weren't; I had traveled somewhere they hadn't, and I was offering something based on that. Whether or not they took me up on the offer—or they already knew about it and had, for example, met the company behind the new technology—they appreciated that I was scouting for them, that when I had a lot of other things to think about, I was thinking about them. We humans are quick to pick up on that. Interestingly, that approach earned me my first stage appearance.

# FIRST MADELEINE, THEN MATTHEW

The first time I ever spoke on stage, I followed Madeleine Albright at a food sustainability conference hosted at the University of Nebraska. When I traveled to that conference, I didn't have a speaking assignment. But my ultimate goal was to share the stage with some of the famous executives—and with Madeleine Albright.

Now, when I arrived, I scoped out the conference organizer and introduced myself. "Hey, I've been emailing with you. I'm Matthew Chang; nice to meet you in person." (Incidentally, he now works at Chang.) I then added, "If you can spare five to fifteen minutes on stage, I've already got a presentation ready, and I'd love to share my view on food manufacturing."

At first, he was too preoccupied to hear me out; he was organizing a conference with VIP speakers. But after a day of conference prep, he turned to me and said, "Look, if you want to go on stage, I've actually got ten minutes following Madeleine Albright. Do you want that slot?"

Absolutely, I wanted that slot. Now, what distinguished me was my attitude: being willing to just go. First off, I brought myself to Lincoln, Nebraska. You don't just happen to be there; you go for a reason. I had corresponded with the conference organizer ahead of time, so I was prepared. And I had my speech ready; I was ready to get on stage. It's likely that any of the other executives there, from some of the country's biggest food companies, would have said, "I'm not ready. I need more time, I need a topic," or, "I need my marketing team to build my PowerPoint." But I was ready. Be ready.

Bringing it back around to mentorship . . . that speech in Omaha earned me a mentor in Dr. Timothy Wei, who at the time was the dean of engineering at the University of Nebraska and was responsible for bringing them into the Big Ten. He's American-born Chinese. Our friendship grew from our first meeting there, and I started supporting him at all of his conferences. And from that point forward, I became part of his inner circle—the group that traveled with him as he took his food sustainability conference on the road. We went to UC Davis, Minneapolis, the headquarters of General Mills, and the National Institute of Standards and Technology. Since Timothy knew I was flexible and always ready, he never assigned me a formal speaking slot ahead of time; he slotted me in once all the more rigid pieces were finalized. After two years and six conferences, I had presented on the future of food manufacturing six times. And at that point, I noticed something had changed—he was coming to me for advice just as often as I was going to him. Because I came from industry and he came from academia, there was a lot I could offer that he didn't see up close.

## SMART WATER, SMART MENTOR

Another mentorship anecdote starts with a company I adore, called PTS, based near Atlanta, Georgia. Their founder traveled with me on several engineering projects in China. He had deep experience there because he had been in Hong Kong during the opening of China, supporting PepsiCo as their first plant manager when they moved across the causeway into Guangzhou to open their first factory.

Very quickly, I realized this man was a bottling expert; his name was Paul Clark. Paul knew more about bottling than anyone I've ever met. He famously developed the Smartwater bottle. Much other modern beverage packaging can be traced back to his perfectionist engineering and his ability to deliver new packaging formats at scale for big brands. Now, Smartwater is significant because that style of bottle created an entirely new category in the beverage industry. Suddenly everyone raced to follow, and now all the premium waters on the shelf owe something to that one innovation. Paul and I developed a rapport through our travels, and though I was just a project manager at the time—and he was the president of his company—he began to funnel most of his correspondence to my company through me, even though technically I wasn't high enough on the org chart for that to make sense.

So, when I finally hung out my shingle and launched my own firm, Chang Robotics, Paul was one of the first people I paid a visit to. I asked him if he'd be interested in having me join PTS as a partner. I wanted to go straight from employee to co-equal, essentially. His response was incredibly telling.

"If you want to become a partner, come to Atlanta and present to our current partners. I'm sure we'll have you on. But I think we'd rather have PTS follow Matthew Chang in whatever you decide to do because I think you'll lift us higher that way."

That boosted my confidence. Here was a guru and legend of engineering—a man who had changed part of the physical world we live in, who had opened markets for international businesses—telling *me* he was more interested in what *I* could build *outside* his business than what I could build inside it.

# MANY MENTORS, MANY BACKGROUNDS

I deliberately chose a diverse set of mentors early in my career. The only rule was that everyone I contacted had to be a professional designer—either an architect or an engineer—who had started their own firm. One of them was a Hakka man, from my father's tribe of Chinese, who lived in Penang, Malaysia (yes, the place where the curry is from at your Asian restaurant.) His name was Lee Mien Chong, and he ran a successful architectural design firm in Penang. He had designed most of the factories for international companies that began offshoring to Malaysia.

Lee gave me brilliant advice when I told him I was thinking of starting my own firm. P*ick a sunrise career.* That line is now in our company's onboarding deck. Now, at the time, I responded, a bit too literally, "Mr. Lee, are you suggesting I go into solar?"

Under his breath he muttered, "You stupid Americans."

"Mr. Lee, help me out here."

He explained, "A sunrise career is one where the sun is just rising, and for your entire career, the sun will burn hot on your back."

*Ah . . . an emerging industry. Thank you, sir.*

That idea—combined with input from my clients—led us to focus on robotics in 2017, well before most firms were even thinking about it. It was that combination of industry foresight and the sunrise theory that pointed us in the right direction.

Beyond Lee, there were also Greg Ellis, Ned Fiss, and Chris Paulsen, each a founder of a firm with a different specialty: industrial engineering, environmental engineering, and automated material handling systems, and more. Looking back, I believe they all had more faith in me than I did. Like I said earlier, I had already experienced four failed business launches. I didn't know what it actually took to cross the chasm, to go from superstar employee to successful business owner. The leap felt huge, too great a gap for me, and I didn't know if I could make it.

Now, what gave me confidence wasn't simply their collective belief in me at a crucial point in my career; it was the fact that all of them had once been where I was. They didn't flinch at the idea of me launching my own firm. They didn't see any reason why I couldn't do it.

In my ten-for-ten mentor experiment, I noticed a pattern: Every one of those business owners started their firm after one of two things happened. Either they were laid off or fired, or they became dissatisfied with how their company was treating clients. In both cases, the spark was adversity—and a greater loyalty to the client than to the employer.

There's another pattern several shared: No seed capital. But all of them had a first client. That's what launched their businesses. Same with my firm, Chang Robotics. We didn't raise money; we just got customers.

## THE HEALTHIEST DYNAMIC

The above is probably why none of these mentors feared I would become a future competitor to their own business. Entrepreneurs, especially self-made ones, tend to be humble. And they're humble because they've *been* humbled. If you've been in business for more than a few years, you know what I mean. There are moments that bring you to your knees. But if a potential mentor is guarded or competitive with you from the start, it's probably not going to be a good match. A successful mentor-mentee relationship requires trust. If it's not there, move on. Someone else will gladly take the call. That kind of person—the one who's *not* trusting—is someone you're just never going to get to the lunch table or the coffee table with. On the flip side, I've found that because of their humility, entrepreneurs are usually very open to giving back. They're some of the most generous people I know—not Silicon Valley marketing CEOs, but real operators. Small and medium-sized business owners who built something from scratch are always giving back. It's a bit like a grandparent relationship. That's a healthy mentorship dynamic. A parent is still actively making their way in the world, still hustling and competing. So when you come along as a younger person, there might be tension or rivalry. It's not always intentional, but it's there.

But a grandparent is removed from all that. Their job isn't to parent you as their grandchild; they're there to cheer you on, maybe offer some sage advice, then head home before "bath time and bedtime." They're not going to do the work. When the taxes hit, or the lawsuit comes, or the client issue explodes . . . your team and your paid advisors will deal with it, not the mentor. They're watching from a distance, offering encouragement and the occasional nugget of wisdom. So if you're looking for healthy mentor dynamics, look for someone at least twenty years older than you—not five years older, not ten. At that point in life, they're less concerned with "beating" other businesses. They've got perspective. They're better with their time, too. If they're already mentoring two or three people, they'll tell you they're full. And if they have space, they'll tell you that too. They're thoughtful with their commitments.

## HOW TO DISAGREE WITH MENTORS

Now, if you ever find yourself disagreeing with a mentor, there's a clear way to handle that. The first rule is: **Never do it live**. Don't argue during the lunch, the coffee, the Zoom call. If you feel in your gut that something's off, or that you're going to go a different direction, the better approach is to listen, nod, and say, "That's a really interesting point. I'm going to research that."

Then, later—maybe a week later—you write to them in a thoughtful and respectful way. You say you've considered their perspective, maybe meditated on it, and that because of some additional circumstances, you're choosing to go another direction. I try to sound like a lawyer when I write those notes—laying out both sides, walking through the reasoning, then explaining my decision. I've never once had a mentor react badly to that.

A good mentor knows you probably have more than one mentor with more than one point of view anyway. It's like getting a second doctor's opinion. You might receive conflicting advice. So be thoughtful. Be respectful. But be honest. Let them know if you're not going to follow their advice. Just don't do it impulsively or in the heat of the moment.

Which brings me to the least comforting aspect of mentorship, which is when it ends.

## WHEN MENTORSHIP ENDS

Sometimes a mentor becomes a grandparent, literally, and their focus shifts. Or they're retiring. Or you've simply outgrown them. In those cases, the mentorship should evolve into a friendship. That's the healthiest outcome.

But if it ends for more difficult reasons—maybe there was a misunderstanding, or the dynamic wasn't quite right—I still believe in ending with class. Write a letter. Send a gift. Express gratitude for the time and wisdom they gave you. That communicates maturity, and if they're a wise person, they'll understand that you've graduated.

I've seen mentorships fail, but only because the mentee was inconsistent. They didn't follow up. They didn't show up. They didn't do what they said they'd do. So if you want a mentorship to last, you know what not to do.

## WHEN MENTORSHIP SHOULDN'T EVEN BEGIN: THE GENDER QUESTION

Matthew, is it OK to have a mentor of the opposite sex?

The last section was uncomfortable; I'll try to make this one less awkward.

Personally, I have a high preference for male mentors because they've walked more of the same paths I have. They've been husbands, fathers, business owners. We share more life context. Women should seek female mentors for the same reason. Life experience overlaps more.

As you might imagine, I, as a man, don't take on female mentees. It's not about capability; it's about boundaries. I'm married. I wouldn't want my wife to feel uncomfortable or suspicious about how I'm spending my time, especially when mentorship is purely optional. It's not worth introducing any uncertainty.

Now, I'm not saying it *can't* be done. Men and women might be able to mentor each other effectively. But if you're going to do that, you need to put guardrails in place. Meet in public. Communicate by email, not text. Always be mindful of how the relationship would be perceived by others. That's the key—*perception*. If someone saw your messages or observed your interaction, would it raise questions?

I do ask women for advice frequently, especially in areas where they have more experience. For example, I'm currently seeking counsel from a female intellectual property attorney. But I don't frame our dynamic as a mentorship. I seek counsel. Collaborate. Build teams. But the deep one-on-one mentorship model, I reserve that for same-gender relationships to avoid complications. Especially for men, the question always has to be, *What would my wife think?* That's the standard. If it would cause tension, even just a little bit, it's not worth it. You don't want your wife to wonder; otherwise, someone might wander.

## WHO NOT TO ACCEPT AS A MENTOR

Before we end on an upswing.

Recently, I met with a well-known retired CEO in Jacksonville. He has a most impressive résumé; he's served on all the various nonprofit boards around town and is deeply respected by colleagues. We met for lunch a few times. He even told me he'd admired me for years, which was flattering. But as we got to know each other, I learned that one of his kids lives in Boston, the other in Denver, and he's in Jacksonville . . . alone in his mansion. That's the opposite of what I want when my children are grown. I want to build a home big enough that all my kids and grandkids can live in it, or at least near it. That's real wealth to me. This man doesn't have it, so I don't want it.

It's OK, necessary even, to disqualify people as mentors if you learn their personal life is not something you want to emulate. They may be wildly successful in business, but if their family is fractured or their children are distant, that's a deal-breaker. I, for one, won't take advice from someone who doesn't have the kind of family life I aspire to.

Now, what about the role of faith in mentorship? Do you have to see eye-to-eye to listen heart-to-heart? No, I don't believe every mentor needs to share your exact faith. **But** . . . I do believe you must be able to openly integrate faith into your conversations. If you're a Christian, it's fine to have a Jewish or Catholic mentor, and vice versa. What matters is that your relationship is open enough that you can tie decisions, dilemmas, and direction back to faith and, as I believe, to Scripture. If you share faith, even better. Open or close your sessions in prayer. Make it part of the rhythm of your conversations. That's how you know it's a healthy, honest relationship.

## MENTORSHIP THE JOHN THOMPSON WAY

There's someone I'd like you to meet who does mentorship so well, he's a one-man case study, and a living embodiment of so much of what we've covered in this chapter.

John Thompson first established himself as one of the top financial advisors at Wells Fargo. While there, he built a strong personal brand and a significant book of business, becoming widely respected in the field. On our topic, the guy is relentless; he's constantly seeking out mentors to deepen his knowledge and sharpen his approach. But over time, he began to feel that even at the top of a major institution, he lacked the tools to serve his clients at the highest level. That realization led him to found Congruent Wealth, a firm with an innovative and much-needed mission: to create fractional family offices for exited founders with net worths between $10 million and $100 million. This segment—too wealthy for retail financial planning but not yet high-net-worth enough for a traditional family office—has long been underserved. John's firm operates in what most of the financial industry considers a no-go zone. That's where he thrives.

Now, John actively recruits mentees. He's aggressive, but in a good way. He constantly interviews new candidates because he wants to find younger people with dreams and ambitions bigger and greater than his. He only wants the best and brightest. Of course, he gives a lot of credit to the mentors in his own life who helped him get to where he is. I should probably tell you right about now that John is one of my mentors. He's also one I disagree with often. But he's relentless in making sure I fully understand his perspective before I go another way. Usually, by the fourth time he's brought something up, I'll say, "John, I hear you. Let me summarize what I think you're saying." I'll give him a paragraph back, and he might tweak or confirm it. Then I'll tell him, "And I'm not going to do that. Here's why." At that point, he'll just put his hands up and say, "OK, it's your business. Your decision." That's the dynamic. He pushes hard, but he respects the final call.

John, like all mentors who do this, get a lot out of these relationships, too. John is intentional about finding younger people so he can stay connected to cutting-edge innovation. He's *giving to give*. So are his mentees.

For example, John recently launched a new website and texted me a preview before it went live. It was very much a financial services website, so I gave him my thoughts.

"John, this is bold. It tells a different story from the rest of the finance world." But then I added, "I know you're not done yet . . ." which is my way of nudging him. I offered some advice about building out the thought leadership section, so he got some free consulting and encouragement from me at that moment. Mentoring the mentor, in a way. That's how you know you're doing it right.

**MATTHEW CHANG**

# CHAPTER 6

# NETWORK AGGRESSIVELY

**E**VERYTHING YOU NEED BUT DON'T YET HAVE — every opportunity, every resource, every open door—is currently in someone else's hands. The question is: *Who do you know, and who do they know?*

This is why aggressive networking is **essential** to the Biblical risk-taker's career, personal ministry, and overall life. The moment you meet someone new, you're not just gaining access to that individual, but also potential access to their entire network—every colleague, client, mentor, investor, or partner they've ever worked with or will. Think of relationships as nodes in a web. With each new connection, your web multiplies exponentially.

Now, most people don't think of networking this way. They see it as a one-to-one exchange. They fear reaching out to strangers. They imagine rejection. They minimize the power of a five-minute conversation. And they stay small, cowardly, and obscure. That is not what I want for you.

If you're willing to get over your fear of initiating new relationships, and if you're bold enough to keep doing it over and over again, you'll soon have more opportunities than you can say yes to. To be blunt, it's hard to overstate the importance of networking. Because especially when you're early on in this risk-taking business, you don't know what you don't know, and you don't know what it is you're missing out on—until you begin to see doors open for you through your network. Then you can connect the dots back and realize, *That would not have happened if I hadn't gone to that event, struck up a chat with a stranger, and made an effort to follow up afterwards . . . even though I felt uncomfortable the whole time.* That changes everything.

## THE TOP 2 NETWORKING BENEFITS

Over time, as you keep networking, you'll find you create a **network effect**. In the tech world, this term explains why platforms like Facebook, X (formerly Twitter), or the iPhone dominate. Everyone's already there. A platform's usefulness multiplies as more people join it. It's not (just) the product; it's the people using it.

The same is true in the real world. The more people know who you are and what you're building, the more your impact (and influence) *multiplies*. Every new contact is a potential messenger for your life's work. People who carry your vision or pitch into rooms you haven't yet entered. People who mention your name when you're not in the room . . . which is when your opportunities start to scale.

Besides network effects, another benefit of aggressive networking is **pattern recognition**. As you engage with more and more people—potential partners, donors, investors, clients—you'll begin to notice patterns. You'll start to sense when someone is bluffing, when a promise is too good to be true, and when someone is the real deal. The only way to develop that instinct is reps. You need enough experience with enough people to know the difference between real and fake.

If you wait too long to build your network, you'll find yourself taking your first big risk without the pattern recognition to protect yourself from fakes, frauds, and failures-in-disguise. Worse, one fake friend or phony advisor can derail your momentum when it matters most.

Networking early and often solves both problems. It multiplies your opportunity and sharpens your discernment, and that's Biblical.

Let me give you a more down-to-earth, engineering-based example of how this plays out. In 2022, I was invited to speak at the Georgia Tech Food Automation Conference. As we've already covered, I had developed a track record as a forward-thinking voice on the future of food manufacturing and robotics. While there, I met a collaborative and likable guy named Mark Joppru, who at the time led robotic innovation at ABB, one of the largest robotics and manufacturing tech companies in the world, with a catalog of over sixty industrial robots.

As we talked, Mark said, "It seems like you could help me build this vision I've got for ABB's future in the industry."

I said, "I'd love to be a part of it."

We followed the usual dance—two Zoom calls post-conference. First he pitched me. Then I pitched him. From there, we slowly expanded our teams in follow-up meetings. Then out of the blue, I got a message from Mark: He was moving on from ABB to become the head of strategic accounts at a company called MIR—Mobile Industrial Robots—the largest autonomous robot company in the world. We hadn't worked together on the ABB vision yet.

He apologized.

"I know you put a lot of thought into ABB," he said. "I'm sorry to disappoint you."

But I wasn't disappointed. I'd always wanted to build a relationship with MIR. Now I had one.

Mark fast-tracked us into MIR's top-tier partnership program based solely on the impression I'd made at that food automation conference. Not long after, he left MIR too, but it didn't matter. The team that replaced him believed in us just as much as he had, based on his referral and the trust he had placed in us.

That single relationship led to MIR granting us special access to their core technology and programming rights. That trust allowed us to reprogram their robotics safety settings—something few companies ever get permission to do—and implement them in the first-ever autonomous hospital in the United States. That hospital project succeeded, and MIR, which had since been acquired by Teradyne (parent company of Universal Robot, the number-one brand of collaborative robots or "cobots"), expanded our Platinum Integrator status to include Universal Robot as well. ABB, the company where this all started, eventually circled back and awarded us their Platinum Integrator status too.

One happy hour beer with a guy named Mark led to a domino effect of partnerships, industry relationships, and high-profile projects. Today, we have account managers at ABB, MIR, Teradyne, and Universal Robot who are fully invested in our success. All of that started with showing up, being prepared, and delivering value . . . and networking aggressively.

# FUNDAMENTALS OF NETWORKING: HOW TO BE LIKEABLE

The first thing you do when you're networking isn't talking, but **listening**. Active listening is a skill. Some people are naturally gifted at it, but many of us have to learn it. I was one of those. So I always start by listening, and then asking thoughtful questions. And not just any questions—questions that actually strengthen the relationship.

When you're speaking to someone with obvious authority or social proof in a room, your questions matter. And there are two types.

The **first** are **adversarial questions**—these show up often in engineering Q&A settings. They're basically heckles in disguise. For example, someone once asked me, "Why would you build this yourself? Why wouldn't you just hire Tesla?" Which, to be fair, is a reasonable question—if you know how to hire Tesla. I didn't. So I built my own solution.

The **second** type of question is a **leading question**. This is what I prefer. These questions position the other person as the hero and give them the chance to shine in front of others. One I asked Mark Joppru during our first conversation was, "This assembly of technology you've put together is impressive. Your vision for where this could go is really inspiring. What are some practical steps I could take to help carry this message forward?"

That's a soft pitch; it's my way of showing I'm willing to contribute to their mission. These types of questions build instant rapport. They let the person show off what they know, make them look good in front of others, and quietly position you as a valuable ally, not a competitor.

Now, when it comes to public speaking events or panels, I've developed a tactic that works almost every time: During Q&A, I **wait**. I have a question ready. Then, as the moderator opens it up, I count silently to five. If nobody raises their hand by the end of that count, I raise mine. About 60 percent of the time, I get to ask the first question that way.

Nobody wants to go first—except me. Most people are still wondering what kind of questions are even appropriate. And when you ask a good, thoughtful question that effectively gives the speaker an extra two-minute extension of their presentation, it breaks the ice for everyone else. The audience wakes up. The questions start flowing. And before you know it, the moderator has to cut it off because they've run out of time.

So, that's the straightforward networking likeability formula:

> Listen closely, ask smart questions that make the speaker look good, and be ready to go first.

After someone has demonstrated credibility in public—whether by giving a talk, receiving an award, or leading a session—I make it a habit to introduce myself. I offer a short, specific compliment on what they said. Then I briefly tell them who I am and what I do, and most importantly, why I'd love to follow up.

And then, I leave. That's the move. Don't stick around. Don't launch into your life story. Don't pitch. Don't tell them all your problems before they've even gotten off stage. That's overwhelming.

Do what George Costanza did on *Seinfeld*: "Leave on a high note."

Most of the time, when you get it right, they'll offer you their contact info—phone number, email, or business card—and they'll want to continue the conversation. But you've got to leave the interaction clean and crisp so they remember you positively and without fatigue.

## ETIQUETTE 101

Highly effective networking is sometimes context-dependent. It's rude to badger someone coming off-stage, obviously, but what else is a *faux pas*? Let's talk about it.

As an example, I attend an entrepreneur's conference once a quarter. The motto there is: *You go too much, too often.* Everyone does it. And it's expected that you lean in, be direct, and push your agenda a bit. People want to feel your *energy*. If you come off soft or meek, they're thinking, *Why are you even talking to me? I don't have any job openings.*

Contrast this with an engineering conference, where I'm surrounded by my professional peers, and I have to tone it down quite a bit. I'm more intentional. Precise. Understated.

That was actually an easy adjustment for me when I became a full-time entrepreneur, because I had already worked across a bunch of different cultures. I had learned French business etiquette. Chinese business etiquette. Malaysian, Singaporean, and so on. I was already used to switching hats depending on the room I was walking into. And in American business, just like in ministry, law, engineering, or healthcare, every domain has its own culture. Knowing your environment matters.

So be intentional. Know what hat you're wearing—and how much forwardness or subtlety the environment calls for. Some rooms speak in riddles. Others speak in commands. In some industries, it's OK—even expected—to leave a little mystery in how you present yourself. That kind of intrigue can actually create follow-up opportunities.

## A PRE-NETWORKING RESEARCH TIP FOR INTROVERTS

Now, for the wallflowers reading this—those of you with social anxiety or introversion—here's a simple strategy to build momentum: Subscribe to your local business magazine. In my city, that's the Business Journal. Every other month they'll publish a list of the "Top X" in various industries: top IT firms, top law firms, top CEOs. My personal favorite? 40 Under 40.

And here's what you do: Find someone on one of those lists and send them a note of congratulations. That's it. Use their website, their LinkedIn, or whatever contact info is easiest to reach. Send a short message that demonstrates some basic understanding of what they've accomplished. That's key. Read their website, skim their posts, and know what you're talking about.

It's the same principle I've experienced on the receiving end. These days, after eight years of building, I've gone from trying to get meetings on people's calendars to trying to keep people off mine. And the people who break through, the ones who get a fast response from me, are the ones who reference something I said or wrote.

They'll message me something like, "I watched a video of yours from last year, and there was something you said that stuck with me. I've been thinking about it all weekend." And then they quote it. To that person, I say, for example, *How can I help you? I've got time next Tuesday. Want to meet in person or online?*

The generosity comes because they did their homework. So if you want to have lunch with a CEO or a senior pastor or some other influential leader, start here:

I listened to what you said, and it had a personal impact on me because . . .

That simple sentence is one of the highest-converting networking openers you can use.

## SOCIAL CAPITAL AND NETWORKING MARINDA'S WAY

We've all met someone who barges into a room and immediately starts talking—self-promoting, overexplaining, trying to "close" people they just met. It doesn't work. Nobody likes that person.

The best networkers bring social capital to the people they meet. Now, what is *social capital*? It's the goodwill, trust, and relationships you already have—and your willingness to spend it on someone else's behalf. It's a currency. And just like with money, those who give generously tend to receive more in return over time. That's why the business development philosophy at Chang Robotics is simple, you know. "Give to give." Not "give to get." *Give to give.* It's generosity bias (again, we borrowed it from that classic book *Give to Get*, but we've made it our own.) We give, expecting nothing in return, and we trust in God's economy that it was a wise investment of our time.

That means when you meet someone, your instinct isn't, *What can I get from them? but How can I help them? What can I share? Who can I connect them to?* Your goal isn't to score a win. It's to build **trust**. You are a bridge to something greater, and when people begin to see you that way, doors open . . . sometimes in ways you didn't expect.

Let me give you a real example. In Jacksonville, I was invited to join a grassroots initiative called the Minority Tech Entrepreneurs Club. It was a scrappy group of engineers, tinkerers, and idealists—not the type of people who had a long track record of startup success. But they had vision, and they were trying to build something real. They just needed some support and credibility. So I said yes. I attached my name, showed up, and gave the group a little more weight in the community.

That decision paid off. Not in the way I expected, but in a way I needed. The woman who had recruited me to the group, Marinda Bottoms, was incredibly driven. She gave up a secure career to pursue her dream of building an innovation economy in Jacksonville. She took the risk. She sacrificed comfort. And she succeeded. Months later, Marinda earned a leadership advisory role in the mayor's office.

At that point, I needed access to the mayor's office. I had a proposal. I had tried before to pitch the mayor's office and couldn't get through. I didn't have the right access. But because I had supported Marinda, because I had been generous with my time and my reputation when she was building her dream—she was now able to open that door for me. And she did.

As destiny would have it, the mayor signed off on my proposal. That outcome started not with a sales pitch or a cold email. It started by saying yes to a group of passionate underdogs who just needed one person to believe in them. That's the network effect in action.

Remember, it's not just about who you know. It's about *what you do* for who you know—and what they remember when they have the power to return the favor.

Aggressive networking doesn't have to be pushy. It's consistent generosity with a healthy helping of pattern recognition. It's treating everyone like someone who might one day be in the room you're trying to get into. And if you treat them that way, you won't need to force your way in. When you *give to give . . . to give some more . . .* the door will already be open.

**MATTHEW CHANG**

# CHAPTER 7

# BUILD YOUR TEAM

**B**Y THIS POINT, YOU SHOULD BE ULTRA CLEAR—crystal clear—mountain-stream level of clear that if you're going to have an eternal impact, you're going to be taking risks in your life's work. Whether that's in ministry, public service, a for-profit corporation, or something of your own creation, risk is unavoidable. And the likeliest path won't be jumping straight into that dream with no experience—planting a church cold, launching a company from scratch, or coming out of college trying to be the Zuckerberg of your space, or dropping out and thinking that alone qualifies you. That template doesn't work for everyone (or most anyone.)

You must first enter the state of preparation. And while you're in that state, there is studying. There is praying. There is serving. These disciplines will spiritually fortify you so that when you move into the next phase—starting small—you're not starting unprepared. Whatever "small" looks like for you, know that you won't ultimately stay there. As you begin, you'll encounter questions you don't yet know how to answer. Then you'll encounter questions you didn't even know you needed to be asking. That's when you'll begin to seek out mentors—people who've already wrestled with what you're just beginning to face.

From there, you'll start meeting more people. And more. You'll experience the network effect. Mentors, peers, collaborators, and partners will multiply. Some of those people will just fit. When you talk about your vision, they're already sharing it. It's like you finish one another's sentences. Your values align; your skills are complementary.

What you may not realize at first is this: *You're already beginning to recruit your A-Team.* This is exactly what Jesus did before he began his public ministry—he gathered his disciples. You may not have realized it, but that's exactly what you've been doing, too. In this chapter, we're going to make that process conscious.

Networking has a purpose beyond meeting the people you've met. From your new primary connections, great friendships form—and can become something more. There is nothing stopping this. We have unlimited freedom in this country to be friends with people, right? Our friendships and affinities are not regulated by anyone—including our current employers. So at a minimum, you should be cultivating friendships with these people, actively sharing ideas. People who work closely with me do that by text message. I probably have fifty different text threads on my phone for different affinity groups—several for humor, several for AI, several for engineering, and several for financial activities like mergers and acquisitions. We're in a constant state of communication, as though we're friends, but also demonstrating how we would communicate as colleagues. It's a mix: personal, funny, and pertinent.

# FRIENDSHIP FIRST, VISION SECOND, FEEDBACK THIRD

As you identify people who could become part of your ideal team, begin by developing a friendship with them. That includes sharing both successes and failures. A really amazing weekend with the family and some cool pictures you guys took? That should go out. Something you're struggling with or praying hard over? Share that with them, too. The highs and the lows—that's what forges the bond that creates a founding team.

Next, the person with the dream—that's you—must take responsibility for the vision. That vision can absolutely be shaped and sharpened by the wisdom and insight of others. One thing my team knows about me is that when I have a heavy decision to make, I'll interview as many as ten different people to get a real 360. I'm constantly expanding that circle of influence—the people I call.

When you're building your founding team, you're using their experience and insight to augment your own. That's what a good leader does. The team is the power—you just happen to be the tip of the spear, the one where the buck stops.

The way you communicate with your co-founders or early team members should demonstrate how you'll work together, how you value their input, and what you bring to the relationship as the initiator and visionary. It should be a virtuous cycle of communication.

And as you stay connected to their personal lives—again, I recommend text messages—you'll learn a lot about their circumstances. Let's say you meet a marketer who may one day become your CMO. You might learn that they're frustrated at work, that a shakeup is coming that could negatively impact them, or that someone else at their company is being advanced at their expense. That's valuable insider knowledge. It may end up helping you recruit them when the time is right.

## HOW LEADERS DEEPEN RELATIONSHIPS, IN BUSINESS AND IN LIFE

To deepen these relationships and cement trust, act as a sounding board for your A-Team for anything they want to consult you on, even in an unofficial capacity. It's very common for me to help people I eventually want to recruit with their job interviews, especially when they're aiming for a more prestigious title or position somewhere else. I'm always available to help them frame themselves well, negotiate executive compensation packages, and present their best angle. I'm constantly supporting people in their careers, and because of that, they tend to develop an almost blind trust in me—that if I ever bring them a career opportunity, it's going to be in their best interest.

This has led to situations where there's a delay—sometimes six months, and in some cases, up to three years—before I can actually hire the person I really want. Because I'm still encouraging them in their own endeavors. If it's God's will, they come back to me. And if or when they do, it's with the confidence that I've helped build them up and stewarded their progress, not held them back.

You see, there are little things you can do that really matter to people. Even boosting someone on LinkedIn, as small as that seems, can make them feel deeply seen. Most people don't have active professional social media profiles, whether it's X or LinkedIn. So when they get public recognition or amplification from someone they respect, it's a big deal. For them, that may only happen once a year.

Another simple task: Invite your new, aligned contacts into your exclusive lifestyle. If you've made it this far in the book, you're starting to develop a bit of an inside-access way of living—things like private speaking engagements, invite-only events, grand openings. The key is to begin including your prospective team members in that world. When they're invited to something you've been granted access to, they get the benefit of networking and exposure without having had to earn that access themselves yet. That builds trust and loyalty.

Next, begin using these prospective A-Team members as internal confidants. Around this point, you're starting to develop business plans, market strategies, or product concepts. Share some of those drafts or ideas with them. Ask them to mark up a document, weigh in on a brand video, or give their honest input. That creates a sense that you're already working together—even though you're not officially working together yet.

That's my magic system: *To start working together before we're actually working together.* It's a trial period where we can learn about each other and sample what it's like to collaborate. What I've found is that the only times I've made hiring mistakes were when I rushed the process. You can't go too slow in hiring; you can only go too fast.

Which brings us to the point of **starting**. In the end, the founder is responsible for creating the marketplace opportunity and generating revenue. You have to be out there selling before you've assembled the full team. Whether it's fundraising to launch a ministry or pitching a new consulting service to land that first customer, you're going to be taking action before you feel totally ready. That's the nature of building something real.

What you can do right now is bring your prospective A-Team founder into a formal working relationship—on a consulting agreement, a side hustle, or a moonlighting basis. We live in the gig economy, so this sort of arrangement is increasingly common and low-risk. It's a great way to begin your first professional relationship.

The most common-sense starting point is what's called an **ICA**: an Independent Contractor Agreement. An ICA is legal in most states—though the rules vary, it's almost universally acceptable. It serves several purposes. **First**, it cements you, the founder, as the contractual and legal authority. You are the company, and you're the one issuing the contract. **Second**, it establishes a trade of value. The prospective A-Team member receives compensation in exchange for their genius, expertise, or time. This builds a foundation of mutual benefit, right from the start. And **third**, it lays out a legal framework for the relationship. That includes essential terms like intellectual property ownership, work-for-hire status, non-compete clauses, and non-solicitation of your team or clients. These terms may seem formal at first, especially if you were "just friends" yesterday, but they clarify expectations and protect what you're building.

Most importantly, the ICA opens the door to deeper conversations about equity and ownership. When you move from casual idea-sharing to a formal agreement, you introduce the concept of value—and the possibility of shared value.

As a founder, you should be open to those equity conversations. When someone starts asking about their stake, it means they're seeing the potential of your vision and imagining themselves as a co-builder. That's a good sign. In fact, these side-hustle or moonlighting agreements are often what move a founder from A to B, from zero to one. They're how you get to the point where you actually have a product, a service, satisfied customers, and even revenue. You're no longer just talking. You're now filing tax returns. You have a real business.

By this point, your side-hustling A-Team member will likely approach you when they're ready to make the leap. That's how it's happened for me.

Every member of the executive team at Chang Robotics and every general partner at the Chang Robotics Fund has been recruited through this exact process. They started on side arrangements—consulting, part-time, gig-based—and then, when the time was right, they came to me ready to commit more fully. That means more time, more responsibility, more compensation, and in many cases, earning equity.

Those are treasured conversations. Because when someone brings that to you, it means they're not just working on your company. They've bought into the vision, and now they want to help build it with you.

Now, let's say it's not quite time to formalize anything legally or contractually. You're not there yet. But you still want to maintain the relationship, build rapport, and keep the door open for possibly bringing someone into your organization down the line. What can you do in that in-between stage?

In my view, it's all about the continuous drip of progress. Professionally, what most people crave—across industries and roles—is to feel like **insiders**. Everyone wants to be part of something. Whether it's being close to the CEO in a large organization or simply being the friend of a risk-taker who's building something bold, people love having that access.

It makes them feel like they're on the inside of something important.

So you want to cultivate that feeling. Create your own mini fan base—or maybe think of it as an informal board of advisors—and keep them updated. Maintain regular contact. Because once you go quiet, people start assuming failure or that things have stalled.

Now, your updates don't need to be huge milestones. In fact, they shouldn't be. Keep it light and steady. For example, you could share the logo you just finalized. That alone can feel like half a company to the average person. Or you might share a draft of your website—something you just threw together, even if it's early. Or maybe you just got off a promising sales call or fundraising pitch and want to share what happened.

This is key: *Whenever you share those updates, ask for feedback; ask for advice.* This draws people closer. You're letting them feel like their input is shaping the outcome of your business, and if they feel that way before they're officially involved, imagine how much buy-in they'll have when they are. You're also demonstrating something crucial—you're a good listener. And as we've already talked about, listening is one of the most powerful relationship builders you have.

That method has worked for me 100 percent of the time. I can't think of a single talented person we've lost while using this approach. As of this writing, I have four people who are top of mind, who are "in the queue," so to speak. They're not on the Chang team yet, but they're getting insider access. I'm already sharing decisions with them. I'm asking for their advice. I'm bringing them into the decision-making process before it's really necessary, and that builds culture early. They start to understand how I work. They feel part of something.

The other thing I do—and I recommend this for any founder—is share internal team highlights with prospective recruits. Once you have more than one person, you have a team, and it helps to make that team visible. Talk about someone's promotion. Share someone's career wins. Let your prospective A-Team see that a "normal person" just like them is thriving with you.

That makes the opportunity feel real. And for many, it's the final nudge they need to say, "I want to do that, too."

## THE PERSON, NOT THE POSITION

Remember, you're looking for the **people** you want in your company, not simply trying to fill a role. You can always hire for a **position**—but even when you think someone fits a label like "accountant," you don't actually know yet if they're the right kind of accountant. Accounting alone has how many subcategories? And someone might be a nice person, but not remotely the kind of agile, tech-savvy, fast-paced thinker you need.

So the question isn't what someone does; it's, *Who are they?* With anyone you want on your team, you're looking for alignment—people whose culture, character, and principles match yours. That is the only thing that truly matters in the early days. Once you have that, you can find the right seat on the bus for them, to borrow that analogy.

If we follow the model Jesus used, that's exactly what he did. The first thing he did was choose the person. He called them by name. He didn't lead with a ten-year vision or an org chart—he simply said, "Follow me." He brought people in from all walks of life—different trades, different ages, and vastly different socioeconomic backgrounds. That was the original diverse organization: Jesus's ministry.

They portrayed Mary Magdalene in the popular series *The Chosen* as essentially a demon-possessed prostitute, and yet she was redeemed and became a trusted member of Jesus's ministry. John, on the other hand, was portrayed as around nineteen years old. Different ages, trades, backgrounds, all coming together to work as one team. Diversity in people, unity in spirit.

That's the model we've followed at Chang Robotics as well. One of our first five employees was an eighteen-year-old intern. A lot of people questioned that choice. But I'd known her for years from student ministry. When she graduated high school, she told me, "I don't know what I'm going to do, but I just want to work for you."

That was enough. We found a seat on the bus for her. Her role changed and evolved over time—as she grew personally, discovered more about herself, and developed new interests. But she started in the culture, and that's what mattered.

That's why we hire aggressively in college. Personally, I don't love hiring recent college graduates. I'd rather hire someone before they graduate and bring them into our culture early. That way, they're not just joining a job, but growing into a mission. Why *before* graduation? Well, when you're recruiting fresh college grads, you're competing against the big W-2 employers—the large tech companies like Honeywell, Rockwell Automation, and consulting firms like Accenture, KPMG, Deloitte, McKinsey. Those are our competitors for talent at Chang Robotics.

And when young grads are in that comparison frame, they start valuing things that actually aren't that valuable. We've had real candidates ask us, "What's your PTO policy?"

We don't have a paid-time off policy. The policy is: *You work really hard when it's time to work hard, and you work a lot less when things slow down.* It's seasonal . . . just like harvest. That's the policy.

But then we'll get the response, "Well, this other company is offering 12.5 days of PTO." We're being measured against something that's not even comparable.

We recently hired a couple of college grads, and one of them told us her decision would come down to our health insurance policy. She was a healthy twenty-two-year-old with four years of eligibility left on her parents' insurance, coverage that's likely far better than anything I could offer through the open market.

What I am offering is responsibility, client exposure, and cutting-edge technology. The real stuff. The kind of substance that makes a young person's career. But what happens in the college graduate market is that people compare HR benefits, not the substance. They don't yet see what actually builds a career. That's why we prefer to hire interns. It's easier to bring interns in, and we're rarely competing with anyone for them. Big companies either have rigid programs or no programs at all. For us, it's common to set up a part-time internship during the school year. They earn some pocket money, we get low-cost labor—and they get exposure to everything we do.

By the time they graduate, they already have an offer for full-time from us. There's no comparison shopping. It's just: *When do I start?* We've usually been working with them for two or three years. We know who they are; they know what they're walking into.

That's why we take this approach. We play the long game.

I'm happy to invest years getting to know someone before placing them in a key role. And yes, part of the reason it works is that we're showing up before anyone else is even recruiting them. We build the relationship before they start comparing offers. As early as freshman year, sometimes even earlier—we're there.

Because parents know we do this, and because department professors at universities know we do this, we have an unending backlog of internship requests. At this point, it's just a matter of choosing the ones we want.

## Cultivating the Next Generation

When it comes to finding these future "disciples" through colleges or universities for your future company or ministry or other endeavor, you can start in two main ways.

**First**, there's the organically grown category—being active in the places where interns already are. One of the easiest and most effective ways to begin is by becoming a "professor for a day." Here's the tip: anyone who offers to teach a class at their local university will be granted a guest lecture. You may not get to choose the exact course—maybe it's international business, finance, marketing—but there will always be a professor looking for an industry speaker to fill a slot. Professors are like podcasters—they're always scrambling to find compelling content for the next class. And this is true anywhere in America. If there's a university, or even just a community college nearby, you can do this.

Once you give a talk, you'll be approached afterward by students. One of them will become your first intern. And as soon as you've hired just one intern from that school, you've established a relationship. From there, it's as simple as emailing the department chair, letting them know you had a great experience and want to do more. They'll start advertising your positions to their students for free—via email lists, campus boards, and other internal networks.

It really is that easy: Offer to teach, deliver your guest lecture, hire one intern, then tell the department chair. From that point on, students will start coming to you.

Every university also has a Career Resource Department. They're another fantastic channel. They'll post your openings and internship ads across campus. And again, it won't cost you a thing. With $0 and just a few hours of effort, you can launch a successful internship program.

If you want to take it one step further, show up at a university career fair. Smaller colleges in particular deeply appreciate employers who show up. They often have limited outside support, so when you contribute in this way, it means a lot. That appreciation translates into long-term access to top student talent.

That's the collegiate circle. Now let's talk about the professional circle—your future co-founders and early employees. This is where things get serious.

Look, 100 percent of zero is still zero. Owning all of something that has no value is meaningless. But if you own 50 percent of a growing company that has real value, that's significant. So I always encourage founders: Be incredibly generous with equity. As generous with equity as you are with financial giving. That same spirit of generosity builds great companies.

At Chang Robotics, we set aside 30 percent of the business's ownership for key executives. These are people we handpicked through the recruiting process I've just described. They knew that by stepping in, they would collectively own a substantial share of the company.

Each one of them received a custom deal. And in the early days of a company, you're free to make those one-off arrangements. You can't do that once you become IBM; too many legacy contracts, too much red tape. But when you're still young and scrappy, you have total flexibility. We've used three tools to structure those deals:

1. Sweat equity
2. Purchased equity at a discount (We sell equity to employees at a six-times discount to make it accessible and meaningful.)
3. SPVs (Special Purpose Vehicles. That's just a fancy way of saying "internal joint venture.")

Say you're launching a business that doesn't yet have an e-commerce branch, and you meet someone who's an e-commerce expert. You can set up an SPV where that person gets 25% of profits from the e-commerce line. Why? Because they're taking the risk to build that arm of the company.

And let me tell you: when you offer something like that to a mid-career professional—someone with ten or fifteen years of experience—they know what's real. They've been through enough HR noise to understand that most corporate perks are fluff. They know all health insurance is mediocre. All PTO is subject to your manager's mood. 401(k)s are often just tax-deferred distractions. None of those HR terms actually matter. What matters to real professionals is:

- Career trajectory
- Lifestyle

- Health
- Take-home pay to their family

So when you offer someone 25 percent of the upside in a growing venture, they're comparing that to everything else on the market—which usually includes zero equity. Even Amazon offers equity only in the form of slowly vesting stock with a three-year lockup. You've just blown that out of the water.

That kind of offer helps them bridge the gap from employee to owner. And that's the only way to level up in a career - owning something.

If you, as a founder, can offer either direct equity in your business or shared rewards through an SPV, you're providing a unique pathway that only early-stage companies can offer.

Now, sure, in ministry this looks different—there's no profit interest. But the principle holds. You can still offer titles, domains of responsibility, and real ownership of outcomes. For instance, you might appoint a young leader as Senior Pastor of digital ministry. That title carries meaning, authority, and opportunity. And it creates that same sense of shared vision and long-term commitment that equity does in the business world.

You're building a fellowship, not just hiring employees. You're giving people meaningful ownership in something new and worth doing. And when you do so, you open the door to extraordinary talent you might never have imagined would work with you.

Case in point: Dr. Timothy "Tim" Wei (pronounced, *way*)

## TEAM-BUILDING TIM'S WAY

Tim is an aerospace engineering PhD from the University of Michigan. He went on to become department chair of engineering at Rutgers, then led the engineering program at RPI, and finally served as the Dean of Engineering at the University of Nebraska. His tenure there coincided with Nebraska's entrance into the Big Ten, and during that period, he oversaw a 250 percent expansion of the engineering program.

He demonstrated excellence at both RPI and Rutgers, which positioned him for the Nebraska role at a pivotal moment in the university's history. While the athletic side of Big Ten membership got the headlines, academically it meant that Nebraska Engineering had to rise to the level of its peers—Purdue, Northwestern, Iowa State—institutions already known for elite engineering. Tim led that transformation. He took the department from forty professors to 140, onboarding 100 tenured faculty. That level of hiring and growth is almost unheard of in academia. These are not adjuncts teaching night classes online. I'm talking about relocating big-name, tenured faculty to Lincoln, Nebraska, and getting them to tie their careers to the university.

To make that happen, Tim had to cast an exciting, future-focused vision. That led him to launch a new thought leadership series—a conference platform to forecast industry needs and rally academia to meet them.

And that's when I met him. He had launched a transformational food manufacturing initiative and gave me my shot at a first public speech in a high-stakes academic setting (remember Chapter 5, "First Madeleine, Then Matthew"?). So I entered his orbit during this high-impact stretch of his career. Under Tim's leadership, Nebraska Engineering became the university's top-ranked department. He didn't just meet the Big Ten standard—he matched the mean of its elite engineering programs. In short, he led Nebraska from zero to hero in just a few years.

It wasn't just hiring; it was the way he *sourced* vision. These summits he hosted brought together academics, futurists, and executives to map out the coming challenges and opportunities in engineering. Now, he didn't necessarily have all the ideas himself. But he built a platform that drew out the best thinking from others, synthesized it, and returned it as actionable insight to both academia and industry. That process created a flywheel effect: *Host summits, publish insights, attract top professors and industry partners, then do it again.* He repeated that model every year until he left Nebraska.

His recruitment into Chang Robotics followed a two-year arc. From the time he announced his retirement from Nebraska to the day he joined our company, I stayed in touch. I kept him updated on the milestones of our young firm, offered encouragement in his own endeavors, and stayed invested in the relationship.

Ultimately, he found the ideal setup—a hybrid model. Northwestern University invited him to be an adjunct-in-residence, giving him office space and access without the full burden of faculty obligations. At the same time, I invited him to become Chief Scientist at Chang Robotics. That gave him the action and innovation of the private sector, partial equity in a for-profit company, and the freedom to work on meaningful challenges.

We created a win-win; I wanted him to keep his academic platform, after all. If Northwestern was his chosen academic home, great. I wanted him to keep teaching. That's part of who he is. It also meant I didn't have to absorb 100 percent of his brainpower; he's a certified genius, and I don't think I could handle that much intellect pointed at me all day anyway. I just wanted a portion of his prowess applied to our most complex problems. So we made it work. We didn't compete with Northwestern; we complemented it. And now, if you search "Chang Robotics" and "Northwestern" together as keywords, you'll see we're the talk of the campus.

This right here . . . this is the magic of long-game recruiting. Team-building. Networking. *Giving to give.* When you stay generous, stay patient, and stay connected, the best people become part of what makes your organization great.

This is startup strategy. It's also Biblical.

Before Jesus began His public ministry, He gathered disciples. He walked into people's lives—tradesmen, laborers, even skeptics—and invited them into something larger than themselves. To do so, He had to possess real leadership attributes. He had to be likable. He had to have *presence*. He had to have social capital.

And He did.

Only after earning that credibility did He share the vision. *Follow Me.*

And they did.

Now, it's easy to understand social leadership in *that* context; the disparity between Jesus and His disciples was immense. But the dynamic is still instructive. The leader casts a vision. The followers gather not because they fully understand it but because they sense the leader is worth following. That's the point—if you want to build a team worth leading, *you must be someone worth following.* That takes clarity of purpose. Humility in your speech. Transparency in your actions. It takes inviting people into something that stretches them, transforms them, and gives their gifts a worthy outlet. When people feel that, when they truly believe they are near something important, they will follow you.

And when you build your company the Biblical risk-taker's way, they'll stay.

# MATTHEW CHANG

# CHAPTER 8

# BECOME FINANCIALLY LITERATE BIBLICALLY

**WHAT WOULD HAPPEN IF EVERY BUSINESS** represented in a church congregation tithed from the business?"

That's the question Pastor Joby Martin once asked me. Reframes everything, doesn't it? How much money can you take to heaven? None. How much of the stuff on earth was here before you were born? All of it. Reframes everything *else*, doesn't it?

Look . . . everything you have—and everything you will ever touch—was here before you, and will be here after you're gone. Maybe the low-cost stuff from your local box store wasn't here in its present form, but the atoms and energy used to make it certainly were. That's the starting point of Biblical financial literacy. You are not the owner; you are the steward. The whole world belongs to God. You've simply been given one lifetime to manage a small piece of it.

This is how I see my finances. Take my house, for example—it's mine to steward while I'm alive. After I die, it will either go to someone else . . . or go to waste. The same is true of everything I've owned as an adult: the money in my bank accounts, the magic internet coins I lost in a boating accident (IYKYK), the surfboards in the garage right now. If it's not eternal, then I'm just a temporary steward. That's why tithing is more than charity, it's a worldview test.

When you're in startup mode, tithing off your first invoice is simple. Right there at the beginning, your income is zero. Then comes your first customer. A positive amount in the business checking account. If you tithe when there's not much to tithe from, it sets the pattern; you're training yourself to give your first and best to God before you've even accumulated much to "lose." Because if you wait until the end of the year, or until you're cash flow-positive or you've reached some magic profit margin, you're unlikely to ever do it.

**Tithing is foundational, not optional. First fruits, not leftovers.**

When we launched our venture capital firm, we wrote it directly into our SEC filings to the effect of, "Before any distributions to partners or profit-sharing, 10% will be tithed." Yep, the lawyers pushed back. "You can't say that," they told me. "Investors might read it." Good. Let them.

Still others worried this would turn off potential capital sources. We moved forward anyway. What happened? We got licensed; the SEC approved us. The result? Investors, partners, even attorneys were *encouraged*. We became a generosity-driven profit engine. And we attracted people who wanted to be part of that. And *only* those people. We even had inquiries from sources like a Saudi family fund (as in, the Kingdom of

Saudi Arabia) and the Bill & Melinda Gates Foundation. I'll use anyone's money to rebuild American industry, but if they have a problem with our commitment to Christian generosity, they're welcome to take their money elsewhere. Simple, really.

What else are we going to do? As another Pastor Jobyism goes, "Your kids are going to buy expensive blue jeans with your money after you're gone."

So what are you doing with it while you're still here? You are either a steward of your money or a slave to it. Get the shackles far away from you.

## HOW TO UNSHACKLE YOURSELF

Recently, I saw a viral post from a highly successful entrepreneur. He had just exited his company and come into millions overnight. I dropped a few replies with advice for him but really, for all reading. Simple stuff. The kind of thing every Christian entrepreneur should already know:

- Tithe your money; tithe your business.
- Tithe on your very first paycheck or invoice.
- Tithing is both obedience and worship.

Now, this isn't a Christian accounting book. But first, understand this: Stewardship is bigger than money. It's all about people. It's about your time. And about how *your* people spend *their* time. At Chang Robotics, we hold ourselves to a 100:10 ratio. For every 100 hours of compensated work, each team member is expected to put in ten hours of unpaid community service. It's not in anyone's employment contract, but it is part of our company culture. When we started the 100:10 initiative, we had 50 percent buy-in; now it's 90 percent. And at our last company survey, our ratio had hit 100:15 of hours worked to hours volunteered—much to my delight and to the delight of our Master.

As of this writing, we have seventy team members across full-time and contractor roles. That adds up to roughly 60,000 paid work hours per year and 9,000 hours of voluntary service, so 69,000 hours annually going toward both kingdom-building and kingdom-serving.

Take one of our part-time employees, for instance. She works twenty hours a week and volunteers eight hours a week reading to children in hospitals; that's a 40 percent ratio. Five of our team members operate at that 40 percent level. Last year, three were at 0 percent. So I called each of them personally. All three made a commitment to change. And as of this writing, all three followed through this year.

We can't talk the walk but not walk it out. And if we're walking, we also need to be talking. That's why we say publicly, on our website, that "Chang Robotics is a Christian organization with a Biblical worldview." That wasn't easy at first, but the fears didn't come to pass. I don't even remember what those fears were, actually. And the fruit has been that our employees *love* it. We take care of them. So they want to take care of the community. See, I don't believe in "spoiling" employees. I want them to *want* to work at Chang. I want them to have capital to start side businesses (they can) and purchase real estate (they do). And I want there to be enough money coming into my people's checking accounts that they can afford luxury family vacations (they can) and install backyard deck pools with all child safety measures (they do.) These spouses and children will never forget Chang Robotics.

OK, that's enough touchy-feely for now. This isn't a math

book, but we all need hard numbers. Rather, concrete ways to deploy our numbers. I'm familiar with two models of radical generosity for yourself, your business, and your employees who tithe. Let's talk about both.

## The Two Core Models of Radical Generosity

First is the **Sustainability Model**. Rick Graham has every franchise he launches commit to a monthly giving subscription to a nonprofit. Not a lump sum. A monthly commitment—10 percent of profits, averaged over the year. Even during debt payoff or seasonal dips, it gets paid. Automatically. No second thoughts. No renegotiations. That discipline creates predictability and strength for the charities they support.

Who is Rick Graham, and what are these franchises, you wonder? Let me tell you more about Rick. He and I run an initiative called Tent Makers, named after the Apostle Paul, who made tents as his trade. The idea is to equip men who want to fund ministry through the marketplace.

Rick's personal story is one of *real* risk. I'm talking lose-your-house risk. See, Rick and his wife Dawn buy Pilates franchises using their own balance sheet. They interview staff. They manage operations. And every time they launch a franchise, they link a charity directly to the business bank account. Every month, a percentage of revenue is automatically sent to the charity . . . no meetings, no approvals, no delays.

They now operate six franchises. Which means six charities receive monthly, stable funding. That allows the nonprofits to hire staff, plan programming, and grow. Their plan is to open one new franchise per year, that means one new non-profit funded per year. That's risk; that's faith.

I get it. Engineers and entrepreneurs alike often struggle with risk. But it's the imagined kind. They run ten steps down a chain of hypotheticals: *What if the prototype fails? What if the website doesn't load? What if someone laughs?* But that's not real risk; that's fear of embarrassment.

Rick and Dawn are living with real risk, the kind where your personal assets are on the line. And yet they keep giving. They believe God provides, and He does. Good stewards not only survive, but multiply.

Alright, now let's take a look at the second generosity model, the **Capital Expenditure Model**. This is our approach at Chang Robotics. We tithe 10 percent of profit after capital expenditures. Since we operate on a project basis, we do our financials quarterly. That means larger checks, fewer times per year. We direct those gifts to local ministries and nonprofits for major needs like vehicles, facility repairs, or tech upgrades. It's lumpy giving with plus-size impact.

And in keeping with this Model are **windfall seasons**. When something unexpected happens—a major client, a big exit, a settlement, a cash spike—we give off the top. Once, we became the single largest donor to the Unsponsored Children's Fund at Compassion International. We got a call from their team. *Would you consider reallocating your gift to our general fund as we are looking to expand our operations?* We said no. We gave that gift to cover the kids on the waitlist, the ones no one else was sponsoring. Then March 2020 came, when churches across America shut down. Compassion asked us how we knew to give. "We didn't," I told them. "We prayed. We felt called. And we obeyed."

This is stewardship - obedience plus generosity plus risk. Be the kind of steward people want to follow, then watch what

God does with what you give—and what *they* do with what you give to them, from what God gives to you. It's Biblical finance. Not addition, multiplication.

**MATTHEW CHANG**

# CHAPTER 9

# PARABLE OF THE RISKS

**JESUS TAUGHT IN PARABLES TO SEPARATE THE** spectators from the serious. And when it comes to the Parable of the Talents—or the Bags of Gold, depending on your translation—it's one of the clearest risk-taking case studies Jesus ever taught.

Let's walk through it. We've got three servants and one master. Each servant receives a sum of money to demonstrate stewardship. The master entrusts these bags of gold to each servant according to their ability. Then he leaves. And here's what's striking: *He gives no timeline for return.* Just as in real life, you don't know how long you've got to work with what you've been given. Could be five years, five months, or five hours. You get the idea.

This parable has been taught as a money lesson, and it is. But it's also a time lesson. The talents are symbolic not just of material resources but of our lives themselves. The master gave them a season—undefined—to act. Two did, one didn't. The faithful stewards, on the other hand, multiplied. They traded. They took risks. They acted before they were told what to do next. And when the master returned, he praised their initiative. "Well done, good and faithful servant." That is the line we're all trying to live for.

With the people I work with and the people I choose to hire, I'm looking for the ones who get this. People who understand that everything they've been given—time, talent, resources, relationships—is on loan. The clock is ticking. What will you do with what's in your hands?

This is a parable first and foremost about the urgency of risk-taking. Let's go to the source to see this for yourself. Here is The Parable of the Bags of Gold in its entirety, from Matthew 25:14-30:

> "Again, it will be like a man going on a journey, who called his servants and entrusted his wealth to them. To one he gave five bags of gold, to another two bags, and to another one bag, each according to his ability. Then he went on his journey. The man who had received five bags of gold went at once and put his money to work and gained five bags more. So also, the one with two bags of gold gained two more. But the man who had received one bag went off, dug a hole in the ground and hid his master's money.
> 
> "After a long time the master of those servants returned and settled accounts with them. The man who had received five bags of gold brought the other five. 'Master,' he said, 'you entrusted me with five bags of gold. See, I have gained five more.'
> 
> "His master replied, 'Well done, good and faithful servant! You have been faithful with a few things;

I will put you in charge of many things. Come and share your master's happiness!'

"The man with two bags of gold also came. 'Master,' he said, 'you entrusted me with two bags of gold; see, I have gained two more.'

"His master replied, 'Well done, good and faithful servant! You have been faithful with a few things; I will put you in charge of many things. Come and share your master's happiness!'

"Then the man who had received one bag of gold came. 'Master,' he said, 'I knew that you are a hard man, harvesting where you have not sown and gathering where you have not scattered seed. So I was afraid and went out and hid your gold in the ground. See, here is what belongs to you.'

"His master replied, 'You wicked, lazy servant! So you knew that I harvest where I have not sown and gather where I have not scattered seed? Well then, you should have put my money on deposit with the bankers, so that when I returned I would have received it back with interest.

"So take the bag of gold from him and give it to the one who has ten bags. For whoever has will be given more, and they will have an abundance. Whoever does not have, even what they have will be taken from them. And throw that worthless servant outside, into the darkness, where there will be weeping and gnashing of teeth."

Now, when did the servant go? "At once." What did they do? Wager it all. That's *risking* it. And *all* of it. Two of the servants doubled their amounts, then gave all the proceeds to the master—because the talents weren't theirs to begin with. Of course, the master rebuked and cast out the fearful servant who buried his share. The two faithful servants got the same reward—to stay in the master's house and have his favor.

There's a real-life parable in the continuing story of Dr. Nahshon Nicks, whom you met earlier. He answered the call to enter public service. Some doors opened, others closed. One opportunity that came to him which he accepted was after-school programs for kids. The need in Jacksonville for underprivileged youth to have somewhere safe to go and something productive to do is staggering.

It came to pass that Nahshon was asked to *double* the number of students in his after-school care. He didn't have money or resources but wanted to accept the opportunity, but what he did have, he used—his network. And so he came to me for counsel. I immediately brought up the parable of the talents; from his reaction, this was a surprise. Which to me, wasn't. This particular parable is generally not taught in the black church because their community is generally subsisting in poverty. So I stumped a pastor, a rarity.

I asked him, "What did the servants in the parable do? Did they pray about it? Post about it on social media? Go through a period of fasting? Those behaviors are all in the Bible. But not on the subject of risk-taking. The servants acted 'at once.'"

Nahshon was uncomfortable. Funding wasn't lined up. Staffing wasn't lined up. He had the opportunity to double his portion.

"Are you going from sixty to a hundred and twenty students today or not? This parable gives you two choices: yes or no."

He said yes; he went at once. Now, he had about ten phone calls to make: his banker, his lawyer, his accountant, and so on. And as of this writing, it's happening. Duval County School District contract is underway. He found the money through donors and bootstrapping, and therefore onboarded the staff he needed. Dr. Nicks' after-school program is the first such Jesus-teaching the county has ever funded in modern history.

The lesson from Nahshon's parable is *not* not to plan. Nahshon did, but only **after** making the decision. Planning is usually an excuse for procrastinating. Get yourself into risk territory, then figure out how to do what you need to do. As Pastor Joby Martin says, "Pray, guess, go."

Let's translate that from preacherspeak. On that ancient middle-Eastern walk to the marketplace, the stewardly servants would have had time to think about what they were going to do. Upon arrival, there would have been some diligence due. Then and only then comes the doing. Which they did. But the first risk was walking there.

This is why I don't like "business planning" because you can't plan for long. As of this writing, the first half of 2025 is almost out, and it's been a wild one: the Los Angeles wildfires, the inauguration of a radically different US President, the announcement of the Department of Government Efficiency (DOGE) and then tariffs followed by trade wars. Plus new physical, kinetic wars. And now civil unrest and violence-laced protest including the assassinations of politicians. And those are just headlines! In any industry there is daily disruption that changes everything. Just get started. Go. "At once." You're plenty ready.

But if you *really* need that last little push (or shove) across the starting line, try making an announcement as your first move. There is an advantage to the flashy press release, which puts pressure on hard. For example, when Amazon announced their drone delivery program, Federal Aviation Administration regulations prohibited such a domestic air delivery service. Drones as an industry were not even ready for such a venture. But Jeff Bezos took the risk; pressure means action, and actions means outcomes. And that's why we're here.

# CHAPTER 10

# THE INTEGRITY INTEGER

**I**NTEGRITY. THE ROOT OF THE WORD IS INTEGER, a whole number. Something undivided. One. That means to live with integrity is to live as one-and-the-same person. So there's not a "Sunday Matthew," a "Weekend Matthew," and a "Workday Matthew," for example. At least, not anymore. That wasn't true when I was younger. Back then, there were different versions of me. Playing sports, partying, living for whatever was in front of me. But over time—becoming a father, a business owner, a community leader—something shifted. I couldn't afford compartmentalization anymore. It's too hard to wear all the hats and play all the different parts. Show up as one: you. The whole you. The integer you.

And so integrity means being your whole self throughout your whole life. Unshackled from expectations. Putting all of you into what you do. It's truth plus maturity. That maturity only comes through trials, usually as a leader. That's when you begin to live aligned with the values you hope others will adopt from you. Not just what you say, but how you live.

For too long, there's been a cultural hangover from the Greatest Generation. That mentality is best described as, "Don't talk religion or politics at work; just show up and do the job." But what that actually bred was a crisis of integrity. Look at Corporate America. Globalist priorities, decisions made in boardrooms that displace local workers. Leaders being told, "Shut up and do what's good for the company, not the people." That's work without integrity.

Living with integrity is the opposite of that, and you have to do that across all areas of life. Say the same thing on social media that you say to your team, to your spouse, and to your pastor. That's the standard. And sure, I'm still a frat boy at heart—I've got the jokes in the private thread in the private chat with my old buddies. But the best of those, I share with my wife, because nothing in my life is so private that it can't handle light.

See, the more aligned your life becomes, the life you're building through risk, the more you'll experience a force-multiplier effect. Joshua Steinman taught me the value of "building in public." That's how he launched Galvanick, his cybersecurity company. He didn't hide the struggle, and I don't either. That's why I "build in public" by, among other things, giving a keynote once a quarter. To an outsider, it looks like constant progress. Prototype one quarter. Yet another new company founded the next quarter. Regulatory approval the next. Fundraising after that. But internally, it's kind of a mess. My inbox tells a different story—one step forward, two steps back. Still, I model transparency, because if your team doesn't see you doing what you said you would do, why should they trust you?

# TRANSPARENCY AS A WAY OF LIFE

I live in Florida under one of the most robust public records laws in the country: the Freedom of Information Act, also called the Sunshine Law. That means every crime is discoverable. We adopt that perspective and repurpose it for how we communicate. I don't want that email an engineer fired off at midnight to become evidence in a future lawsuit when the opposing side's counsel takes us into discovery. So we talk face-to-face. Get it out. Clear it up. Build in public. *Be* in public. Because that's how you act with integrity.

*Dilbert* creator and *New York Times* bestselling author Scott Adams lives just about his entire life in public, pivoting out loud, sometimes to the chagrin of his fans. But that's the deal . . . you will be criticized. Not everything you build will last. But when you fail honestly, you earn more respect than if you had hidden the struggle. That's integrity too. Failures with transparency are invitations for others to rally around you. In Silicon Valley, they say "fail faster." At Amazon, it's "fail cheap." I like both. Experiment, but be smart. Don't go broke chasing the lesson. *Fail fast, fail cheap.*

What can never fail, however, is your integrity-resultant transparency. Here's what you'll realize sooner or later: *You can't partition your life.* Founders don't work eight-to-five and then go dark nights and weekends. Pressure doesn't clock out. Trying to act like it does, changing hats every few hours, is mentally draining. That's why "hot mic moments" are such a liability; they reveal the disconnect. The version of you when the camera's off versus when it's on. Same in VC boardrooms, where founders perform charisma for investors. But it's just that, a performance. And performing all the time wears you down. I can't afford compartmentalization anymore. It's too costly. And for what benefit?

## WEALTH AND THE COMPANY OF ONE

In the interest of upholding my own integrity, let me share with you two quiet struggles I've been having that belong in the public eye—starting with yours. Those two struggles are two words: *company* and wealth.

What is a "company," really? Is something a business, or is it just a department of another business? Where's the line? I'm still not sure I know. Which is strange, considering I currently own seven or eight companies (I'm beginning to lose count.) And yet entire industries, entire economies even, are structured around this construct of the company. People put all their faith and value in it. Banks do. Insurers do. Investors certainly do. But at the end of the day, a company is just a fictitious legal structure. It's not a person, it's not a soul. It's not even a thing; it's paperwork.

When I look at what makes up a company, it's really just **people** and **ideas**. Sometimes assets, like real estate or equipment. But if you take away the good people, is the company still valuable? Not in any real sense. Yet it's rarely reflected that way on paper. That tells me there's a disconnect between this construct and reality. I've been wrestling with that.

Lately though, there's been a second word I can't shake: wealth. Where I live, we're surrounded by it. Wealth management firms. Certified guys who draw up financial plans. Advisors for high-net-worth families. Everyone is talking about generational wealth with buzzwords like foundations, tax shelters, estate planning. It's practically a religion of its own. And it made me start asking the same kind of questions I asked about companies, "What even is wealth? And why do we care so much? Why do we put our smartest, most diligent minds to work helping people grow and protect something they can't take with them?"

As Christians, we believe nothing material goes with us when we die. Not the house. Not the cars. Not even the Bitcoin on your cold wallet. Everything on earth was here before we were born and will remain after we're gone. Sure, we can reshape and repurpose matter; we can turn minerals into steel and steel into bridges. But when I look at the bridge, I still see dirt from the ground, rearranged—also built with energy, from the ground. There's nothing new under the sun.

So if you can't take it with you, and if in the end, you either find yourself in eternal communion with God or eternally cut off from Him, then who cares what your heirs do with your estate? If you're in Hell, your family's trust fund doesn't matter. If you're in Heaven, it matters even less . . . you're beholding the face of your Creator.

Yet Christians fixate on wealth. We all do. Even measure our success in terms of how much of it we accumulate or leave behind. But Scripture is clear: The one thing you *can* take to Heaven is people. That's the only eternal asset.

So if you're trying to figure out whether your purpose on earth is meaningful, here's a solid litmus test: *Will it bring more people with you to Heaven?* That's the only return on investment that really matters. And I'm going to live with integrity so everyone I come in contact with knows I truly believe that.

**MATTHEW CHANG**

# CHAPTER 11

# CHRISTIAN PRINCIPLES WHEN THE GOING GETS TOUCH

**DEAR JESUS... MAY I GLORIFY YOU, AND THROUGH** my actions, lead others to Your name.

This is the essential prayer when the going gets tough, whether it's bad finances, threats of lawsuits, broken relationships, or all of them all at once. Pain is not optional; suffering is. Glorifying God and exemplifying God is how you endure the former without falling into the despair of the latter.

First- or second-year business success usually brings with it a different kind of problem: maturity. Specifically, the maturity required to handle scaling. The pivots begin—and there are always more to come. At Chang Robotics, our pivots have included strategy shifts, staff changes, and operational overhauls. That's normal.

Inevitably, issues arise. Four years into the business, we

had zero debt. Sounds great, right? But here's the downside: we also didn't have any mature banking relationships. I hadn't built a track record with our bank, which meant that if I suddenly needed access to capital to fund a large project upfront, I would've been out of luck. Every major, even highly profitable, company carries some form of debt. Then come the legal challenges. These usually show up around year two or later. Most new founders don't even have an attorney on retainer—let alone the multiple specialized attorneys you'll need as the business matures. For our first five years, we had no lawsuits. Not one. We didn't even need a lawyer. Then in 2022—year six—we were hit with four separate federal lawsuits. Since then, none. But that year taught me a lot. Were we in the "right" on all six of them? I like to think so. In the end, the judge agreed with us. But that doesn't matter when you're in the middle of a lawsuit; it still robs you of your sleep, peace, and a little piece of your soul.

So how do you prepare yourself, as a Christian business owner, to glorify Christ in the midst of adversity—whether it's debt, litigation, failed partnerships, difficult employee terminations, or whatever else comes your way? Because all of those are byproducts of success. They are growing pains. That little prayer will help you big time.

Take a look at the number of active lawsuits involving well-known, respected companies. Every other billboard you pass, there's a picture of a tough-looking attorney just looking for someone to sue. So just because you *are* being sued doesn't mean you're a scammer. What matters is how you respond. Whenever adversity hits, glorify God in your actions from that point forward.

There are trials and triumphs in every story, as are there

temptations also. Wisdom dictates foreknowledge of these so you will not fall prey to them. Have a template for handling a crisis before it becomes one. Fortunately, the New Testament has just that.

# THE BIBLICAL WAY TO HANDLE CONFLICT

In Matthew Chapter 18, Jesus lays out a process for de-escalation and reconciliation. If you've got a problem with your brother, go talk to him—face to face. That's what Scripture teaches. If that doesn't resolve it, then bring it before other Christian witnesses. From there, it escalates gradually and biblically. That's where my head goes first whenever there's conflict: Follow the Biblical model for dispute resolution.

But if that doesn't work—if the other party breaks outside the paradigm of Christian resolution, if things move from amicable to adversarial—then you fall back on the secular approach. That's when legal action becomes the final option. A lot of people don't understand this progression. They want to go straight to the contract or lawsuit. But in my experience, if you've had to bring up the contract, you've already lost. If you're invoking legality to remind someone of the agreement, the relationship is already broken. In your business, you've probably seen this too—once lawyers get involved, the trust is gone.

Another thing I push for, especially from my time working in government, is what we in Florida call the Sunshine Principle. If any text, email, or message you've ever sent were published on the front page of a newspaper, would you be okay with your friends and family reading it? Would you be proud of what you said?

So when the Bible isn't crystal clear—for example, how to handle someone who violated your intellectual property—pray about it. Pray when it's hard, when you're not sure what to do. Then go through and run up the Biblical escalation ladder—attempt Christian resolution. And all the while, act like everything you say and write could one day become public. Because in litigation, it often does. Every email, every text, and every call log can be requested in discovery. You see this happen publicly to people all the time. If you moderate your tone, your words, and your actions with that awareness, you'll avoid inflaming tensions. You'll resolve more things peacefully.

Christ was a peacemaker—*blessed are the peacemakers*—but He also didn't shy away from conflict when it was righteous. He battled the Pharisees, rebuked Satan, and stood before Roman authority with truth. That's our challenge as Christian leaders, to fight for the win we're called to pursue, but also to conduct ourselves with respect, integrity, and grace, even when the other party does not.

That's how we glorify Christ when the going gets tough.

And it *will* get tough.

# CHAPTER 12

# PLAY IT FORWARD

**Y**OU'VE MADE IT; CONGRATULATIONS. NOW IT'S your turn to help others make it, too. You networked with others to get where you are. Now it's your turn to be available. To mentor. To give back. You freely received; now freely give. As we say at Chang Robotics, "Give to give." Not for a return. Not for influence. Just to give.

That reminds me. Back in the 2010s, there was this movement among executive coaches and management consultants to promote "servant leadership." But they stripped Christ out of the concept, and thus the result became hollow. It didn't make sense anymore.

"If there's anything I can do to help you, just let me know," said a boss I once had. So I took him up on it. I walked into his office. I needed to leave by 6:00 PM, but had work that would take until 9:00 or 10:00 at night. He took the work off my desk and helped me that evening, but he never asked again. They never do.

That's the problem with Christless servant leadership: It's signaling, not substance. It lacks the foundation that makes the whole thing work. If you're well off, you should literally be investing in other people with cash. At my company, we currently own eleven startups. I personally own five more. What that means is that when an entrepreneur came to us with a real need—one that we believed in—we were able to meet part of that need by writing a check. That's investing in others.

In addition to financial investments, there are relational and reputational investments too. Say you're a nonprofit founder. You can also serve others by joining their board. Lend your time, your wisdom, and your credibility. When your name and face show up on that website, it communicates something to others. You now have governance responsibility, even advisory responsibility. You're standing beside that mission.

## THE GIVER'S GIVER: MIKE'S STORY

A man I know who knows how to play it forward (and does) at the highest level is Mike Calhoun, founder of Board of Advisors. He is the giver's giver. Mike runs a very expensive, members-only entrepreneurs club. That's his day job—he makes money by selling memberships to entrepreneurs who want to be part of that network. But what I really admire about Mike is that he's the consummate connector. He's always looking for ways to add value to others, whether they're paying members or not. Even if someone used to be a member and left, he's still trying to help. He's one of those super-connectors who's always thinking, "I know someone who could help here," or "You just said something that reminded me of someone who could make that happen."

Mike pours a tremendous amount of energy every day into helping other people. And honestly, you look at his calendar and wonder, When does he have time to do his actual job? He produces four-day conferences multiple times a year—which is a full-time job all by itself—but he's still constantly connecting people, creating value, and helping others. I'd estimate that only about a third to half of what he does is monetized. The rest? It's just giving.

At Chang Robotics, we've tried to formalize that same posture of generosity into a few core practices. Yes, we tithe—we are a tithing company. We've also committed to "second fruits," meaning when we receive unexpected profits, we go above and beyond our tithe to give even more. And our team gives their time too. We ask employees to dedicate 10 percent of their billable hours toward community service. It's not legally enforceable—it's a culture, and it works.

So what does this look like on an individual level for the risk-taker, the founder, the leader? As your business grows and becomes sustainable, you'll have new opportunities to look for financial partners—meaning nonprofits and ministries you can support. You'll also face new levels of accountability. As your name becomes tied to the organizations you support, your gifts become public. You'll be listed on donor rolls. Your logo might show up on their website.

That's why I strongly recommend that leaders—especially Christian business leaders—join one or two nonprofit boards. Every 501(c)(3) organization is required to have a board, and this is a chance to give not just money, but guidance and strategic leadership in helping others build something meaningful and sustainable, just like you did.

I also believe every leader should actively cultivate a pipeline of mentees. Earlier in your journey, you were looking for mentors. Now you should be doing the reverse, identifying and investing in young or emerging talent. You don't need a fancy program to do it; just look for people you can help grow.

One easy way to find mentees is to plug into a local university. Once your business is stable and growing, any business school or department would be glad to have you guest lecture. Even just one class per semester gives you visibility, and professors are always looking for real-world practitioners to show their students how it's actually done.

Another way to connect is through youth-focused events in your industry or niche. At Chang Robotics, we've long sponsored local robotics competitions and student pitch contests. In 2024, we partnered with the Jacksonville Jaguars to host a student business pitch competition. We brought together students from the University of Florida, Florida State, Jacksonville University, University of North Florida, and Flagler College. We loved every minute of it.

What struck me most about the student pitches was how big and imaginative their ideas were. They hadn't been beaten down by the real world yet. They didn't know all the steps they skipped—fifteen, twenty steps from pitch to execution—but they were passionate, compelling, and bold. I wanted to invest in every single one.

By sponsoring events like these, we democratize access. We don't care where you go to school. Last year, the winner came from Flagler—a David beating the Goliaths of FSU and UF. And now we've got relationships with students from each of those schools, who could become mentees.

So whether it's teaching once a semester, attending a K-12 career day, or sponsoring local competitions, there are simple ways to keep investing in the next generation. It keeps you grounded, too. You don't want to get successful, climb your ivory tower, and lose touch with the culture.

Stay connected to the young. That's how you stay connected to the world.

And to close out this book, I'd like to offer you a few ways to stay connected with me.

At **Chang Robotics** (www.changrobotics.ai), we build cutting-edge robotics and engineering solutions tailored to your workforce—whether you're in manufacturing, government, high tech, healthcare, or elsewhere. If that's your organization, we may be able to help you solve your most pressing and sophisticated engineering challenges.

We're also working on a special American-made investment opportunity at the **CR Fund** (www.cr.fund). We are America's premier manufacturing-tech venture capital firm, backing the future of American industry with a focus on robotics, automation, energy, and industrial applications of AI. Everything we invest in aligns with the principles of this book.

And finally, you can follow me on X, formerly Twitter. Look me up at **@matthewachang**. If you liked this book, you'll love what you see there.

So this book is not totally over; it's our ticket to what's next. In these pages, you've seen how faith, risk, leadership, and vision can shape lives, build companies, and serve communities. Now it's your turn. Whether you're an investor, a builder, a founder, or someone still weighing your first leap, there's a place for you in what we're building. Get in the fight. Put your talents to work. Steward your resources well. And live your one lifetime with boldness, integrity, and purpose. Above all, seek risk. Take it. That's the Biblical way.

**MATTHEW CHANG**

# APPENDIX

## Stay Connected & Give Back
## Our Companies

| | |
|---|---|
| Chang Robotics | Innovative engineering firm that provides cutting-edge autonomous robotics tailored to workforce needs. |
| | https://www.changrobotics.ai |
| Curabotics | Curabotics streamlines hospital operations with a Nurse Assist Bots that deliver supplies, meds, and linens - freeing nurses to focus on patient care. |
| | https://www.curabotics.com |
| KodiakTech | KodiakTech delivers American-made, low-emission snow blowers and heavy-duty systems. |
| | https://www.kodiaktech.io |
| GoEco | A revolutionary food packaging solution from Chang Robotics that eliminates PFAS and plastic. |
| | https://www.go-eco.solutions |
| Chang Robotics Fund | America's Premier Manufacturing-Tech VC |
| | https://www.changfund.com |
| AIM | AIM backs U.S.-built manufacturing tech – reshoring jobs, fortifying supply chains, and giving investors a front-row seat to the next wave of manufacturing and energy innovation. |
| | https://www.aimcompany.us |

## CONNECT WITH THE AUTHOR

| | |
|---|---|
| LinkedIn | https://www.linkedin.com/in/matthewachang |
| X (Twitter) | https://x.com/matthewachang |
| Chang Robotics LinkedIn | https://www.linkedin.com/company/changrobotics |
| Chang Robotics Thought Leadership | https://www.changrobotics.ai/thoughtleadership |

## KEEP THE MOMENTUM – SUPPORT THE PEOPLE & CAUSES FEATURED

The risk-takers mentioned in this book are building change every day. If their work moved you, take a minute to connect and, if you're able, donate to support their mission.

| Distinguished Risk-Taker | Missions |
|---|---|
| Tammie McClafferty, CEO | Lifework First Coast (https://lifeworkfirstcoast.com) – a faith-based leadership program that equips Christian marketplace leaders on the First Coast to integrate faith with work and transform their cities.<br><br>Donate here: https://lifeworkfirstcoast.com/donate |
| Roland Udenze, AIA Visionary Architect | LinkedIn: https://www.linkedin.com/in/architecturebyrolandudenze |

| Distinguished Risk-Taker | Missions |
|---|---|
| Rick Graham, Board Member | The Okoa Refuge (https://www.okoarefuge.org) – a Christian nonprofit in Uganda focused on stabilizing families and transforming communities, including programs that rescue and restore survivors of human trafficking. |
| | Donate here: https://www.okoarefuge.org/ways-to-give/sponsor-a-need |
| | Seamark Ranch (https://www.seamarkranch.com) – a faith-based children's home on a 465-acre campus in Northeast Florida, providing a nurturing family environment, education, and life skills for children from families in crisis. |
| | Donate here: https://www.seamarkranch.com/donate-today |
| Mike Calhoun, CEO | Board of Advisors (https://www.boardofadvisors.com) – an exclusive CEO and entrepreneur community/mastermind that hosts high-level quarterly events to connect "disruptive" business owners for strategic growth and partnerships. |
| Marinda Bottoms, Community Ambassador | LinkedIn: https://www.linkedin.com/in/marinda-bottoms/ |
| Timothy Wei, Chief Scientist | GoEco (https://www.go-eco.solutions) - A revolutionary food packaging solution from Chang Robotics that eliminates PFAS and plastic. |

| Distinguished Risk-Taker | Missions |
|---|---|
| John F. Thomson, Owner | Congruent Wealth (https://congruentwealth.com) – a Jacksonville-based boutique wealth management firm that offers "family office-style" services - coordinating investment, tax, estate, asset-protection, and charitable planning for entrepreneurs and families. |
| Ronald Armstrong, Executive Director/Founder | Sponsored by GRACE (https://sponsoredbygrace.org) – a Jacksonville-based Christian nonprofit that empowers children and families by sharing the Gospel, connecting them to a local faith family, and meeting practical needs.<br><br>Donate here: https://sponsoredbygrace-bloom.kindful.com |
| Joshua Steinman, Co-Founder | Galvanick (https://www.galvanick.com) – a cybersecurity company that provides an industrial/OT platform, delivering holistic visibility and threat detection for factories and critical infrastructure. |
| Dr. Nahshon Nicks, Founder | Team Nitro MMA (https://teamnitromma.com) – an organization that builds youths' social, emotional, academic, and leadership skills through mixed-martial-arts training and mentorship<br><br>Donate here: https://teamnitromma.com/getinvolved |
| Joby Martin, Executive Pastor | The Church of Eleven22 (https://coe22.com) – a church movement based in Northeast Florida that helps all people discover and deepen a relationship with Christ through worship, disciple-making, and serving.<br><br>Donate here: https://coe22.com/give |

# ACKNOWLEDGMENTS

There are so many people that I'd like to acknowledge as being part of my story and who helped me write this book, but I can't list them all. I'd like to acknowledge my business partners, Kate McAfoose and Ross Barnard, who have trusted me with their careers for nearly a decade. Also, my colleagues at Chang Robotics, who have accomplished so much. Without you all working so hard and so smart, I couldn't take the time needed to write a book! Finally, I'd like to acknowledge Joby Martin and the Church of Eleven22. It's been a major source of joy and adventure for me to get to be a small part of the Jesus Journey you're building in Jacksonville, Florida.

# ABOUT THE AUTHOR

Matthew Chang, P.E., a visionary leader with two decades of experience, founded Chang Robotics in 2017. Chang Robotics has become known as one of the best firms globally for autonomous robotics and "cobotics," collaborative robots that work alongside and support human employees. Matthew's role at Chang extends to conceptual engineering, program direction, and strategic partnership development, highlighting his adept leadership. He also serves on the board of Lifework Leadership and Jacksonville University and is Chairman of the Board of electric vehicle startup Kodiak Technologies.

Matthew founded the Jacksonville Venture Competition to catalyze a startup ecosystem in Jacksonville, Florida, and has also led the organization of Jacksonville's innovation hub that includes FSU, JU, UNF, FSCJ, and many great local companies and civic organizations. Beyond his professional and service endeavors, Matthew finds fulfillment in surfing, quality time with his children and spouse, ministry work, mentorship, and travel with family. Learn more about his latest projects at www.changrobotics.ai.

www.ingramcontent.com/pod-product-compliance
Lightning Source LLC
Chambersburg PA
CBHW030454100526
44580CB00010B/129/J